McMorran & Whitby

Twentieth Century Architects

McMorran & Whitby

Twentieth Century Architects

Edward Denison

THE
TWENTIETH
CENTURY
SOCIETY

ENGLISH HERITAGE

RIBA Publishing

In memory of my Grandma

© Edward Denison, 2009
Published by RIBA Publishing, 15 Bonhill Street, London EC2P 2EA

ISBN 978 1 85946 320 8

Stock Code 68621

The right of Edward Denison to be identified as the Author of this Work
has been asserted in accordance with the Copyright, Designs and
Patents Act 1988 Sections 77 and 78.

British Library Cataloguing-in-Publication Data
A catalogue record for this book is available from the British Library.

Publisher: Steven Cross
Commissioning Editor: Lucy Harbor
Series Editors: Elain Harwood and Alan Powers
Project Editor: Susan George
Copy Editor: Ian McDonald
Designed and typeset by Carnegie Book Production
Printed and bound by The Charlesworth Group, Wakefield

RIBA Publishing is part of RIBA Enterprises Ltd.
www.ribaenterprises.com

Front cover photo: City Police Station, Wood Street, London, 1959–66
Back cover photo: The 'Gate of Honour', Cripps Hall, Nottingham, 1957–9
Frontispiece photo: McMorran & Whitby's idiosyncratic rustication on the
City Police Station, Wood Street, London, 1959–66

Foreword

The history of architecture is seldom simple, though ideologues may believe otherwise. In any period, new ideas and fashions coexist with older ways of doing things. We can now see that the history of the second half of the 20th century in Britain did not consist of the simple story of the triumph of Modernism, for more traditional ways of designing carried on somehow in the difficult conditions after the Second World War. But though hostilities were certainly declared, there was no 'Battle of the Styles' like that of a century earlier. Those who fought for the continuing value of the classical tradition were hampered by the fact that the Modernists had captured both the institutions and the press. They designed and built as if in a void, for their works were hardly ever published – and if they were, it was usually to be sneered at by those convinced of the moral rightness of the Modernist orthodoxy. Only now is it clear that in the 1950s and 1960s there were, in particular, two designers who demonstrated that it was still possible to meet present-day needs with an architecture rooted in sound structure and experience but which was not, like so much 'traditionalism', feeble and pedantic. They showed that the classical language could be simplified and adapted without losing its vitality and humanity. Their names were Donald McMorran and George Whitby.

I first became aware of their late London buildings: the urbane City of London police station in Wood Street and the extension to the Central Criminal Court in Old Bailey. The latter was particularly impressive for the way it sympathetically added to Mountford's exuberant Edwardian Baroque in a powerful abstracted manner, full of resonances of such heroes as Lutyens and Vanbrugh. I wanted to know more, especially as I found that the late John Brandon-Jones, that continuing conscience of the Arts and Crafts movement, admired and defended McMorran & Whitby's thoughtful and original approach. I began to do some research, greatly helped by getting to know McMorran's art historian daughter, the late Susan Beattie, and then, later, Whitby's engineer son, Mark. But when I offered an introductory article about these intriguing masters of what I saw as a 'progressive classicism', the idea was immediately rejected by the *Architectural Review* and the *Architects' Journal* and treated with polite indifference elsewhere. In the event, my article was published in 1991 in, of all places, *Modern Painters*.

Then (as now?), architects and critics seemed to like polarities. Buildings had to be categorised as modern, and therefore approved of, or traditional, and therefore reactionary and bad, or possibly just eccentric and curious. The notion that there could be an architecture that was at once traditional and modern, and classical without being covered in pediments and pilasters, was clearly incomprehensible. But it should not have been. The early 1970s was a crucial period, as the Modern Movement was then under sustained attack for its perceived arrogance and facelessness. The time was ripe for a modern architecture that was solid, humane and resonant, sustaining the best of tradition – and McMorran & Whitby had suggested a way forward. But Whitby died in 1973 (as did that other would-be progressive Classicist, Raymond Erith), while McMorran had departed the scene eight years earlier. Unfortunately, the void they left was filled not by intelligent disciples but by younger advocates of 'Real Architecture' who thought it enough to deck out their pedestrian designs with Palladian trappings. And then a disillusioned public was palmed off with the facile historicist veneer of Postmodernism.

It was also in 1973, just two weeks after Whitby's death, that a massive IRA car bomb exploded outside the brand new Old Bailey Extension. I remember visiting the scene a few days later, delighted to find that while every pane of glass on the tawdry modernist 1960s commercial block opposite was smashed, leaving it a total wreck, McMorran & Whitby's stone front appeared virtually undamaged. This was, of course, a rather extreme test. But it is also worth observing that while so many of the much-vaunted experimental masterpieces of post-war British Modernism have required hugely expensive revamps to keep them in use, the solid, considered masonry buildings of McMorran & Whitby have weathered well, require little maintenance and continue to give pleasure to their users – as well as to a wider public. Giving satisfaction to clients is an important, albeit unglamorous, aspect of architecture that is too often ignored.

The buildings of McMorran & Whitby have much to teach those with eyes to see and who have a concern for real architectural integrity. They are increasingly admired and English Heritage, with sound historical sense, has listed several of the best. It is also appropriate that this book is in a series on twentieth-century architects published in conjunction with The Twentieth Century Society, for since its foundation in 1979, the Society has insisted on plurality and been interested in good architecture in any style and not just Modernism.

By ignoring fashion, those two brave architects demonstrated that architecture need not be polarised; that it is possible to have a humane, sustainable, creative modern architecture with traditional virtues: a classicism that does not ape the past but is a living expressive language, able to respond to modern conditions. It is our loss that, in recent years, so few have followed this path.

Gavin Stamp

Acknowledgements

First and foremost, I wish to thank my family to whom I owe everything: Guang Yu, Xiao Yu and George, and my mother, father and sister, Eleanor, John and Alice, without whom this piece of work would not have been possible. I wish also to thank Alexander McMorran and William McMorran for their constant and kind support, invaluable insights and criticisms. I owe Susan Beattie a debt of gratitude for instilling in me an appreciation for studiousness and especially so in architecture, though I could never hope to match her high standards. I am indebted also to her daughter, Alexa, for her help and guidance, since she, like her mother, is a writer of the highest order. The same can also be said of Meg Cox, to whom I am most grateful for her expert editorial inputs.

Thank you also to Mark Whitby for his encouragement, and to his mother Charmian for sharing her recollections – and indeed to all members of the families that form the focus of this book, especially the venerable 'centurion', David Farquharson. I owe much to the very many people and institutions that helped to provide material to enrich this book: Betty Murray, the linchpin among the North Audleyites; Elizabeth Stephenson; Betty (Irene) Smallwood; The Royal Institute of British Architects and the staff in their photographic and drawings collections, especially Robert Elwall; The Victoria and Albert Museum; The Royal Academy, including Neil Bingham and Mark Pomeroy; the staff at the Old Bailey, including Stephen Jones; the staff at Wood Street Police Station, including Roger Appleby; the Art Workers Guild including Monica Grose-Hodge; the staff at Suffolk County Council, including Ed Button; the staff at the University of Nottingham, including Jayne Amat, Gethin Roberts and Sue Daley; the staff at Devon County Hall including Charlie Bottrell and Richard England; Jeremy Gould for sharing his expert knowledge of Devon County Hall; Helen Holyoak and everyone at The King's School, Chester; Caroline Stockdale at York City Archives; Adrian Forty for his patience and guidance; Alan Hollinghurst for so graciously enduring research rambles and conversations; Frank Pattison for his translations; Gavin Stamp for having such unreserved faith in McMorran & Whitby's work for so long, and for doing so much to uphold it despite being so often confronted by institutional indifference; Nick Holmes for illuminating so exceptionally the comparatively unknown world of E. Vincent Harris; Alan Powers and Elain Harwood for their enthusiastic support and extensive editorial inputs; Margaret Richardson for her constant encouragement; and Posy Simmonds for understanding and exposing the joys of Wood Street Police Station better than anybody. Finally, thank you to all those at The Twentieth Century Society, English Heritage and RIBA Publishing for dedicating so much time and effort to producing this book and the series in which it forms just a part – not least to Lucy Harbor, Susan George, Anna Walters, Ian McDonald and Matthew Thompson for their generous support.

THE
TWENTIETH
CENTURY
SOCIETY

Without the Twentieth Century Society an entire chapter of Britain's recent history was to have been lost. It was alert when others slept. It is still crucial!

Simon Jenkins, writer, historian, journalist

Love it or hate it, the architecture of the twentieth century has shaped our world: bold, controversial, and often experimental buildings that range from the playful Deco of seaside villas to the Brutalist concrete of London's Hayward Gallery.

Arguably the most vibrant, dynamic and expressive period of architecture in history, the twentieth century generated a huge range of styles. You don't have to love them all to believe that the best of these exciting buildings deserve to be protected, just like the masterpieces of the Victorian era that many likewise once thought to be eyesores. Buildings that form the fabric of our everyday life — office blocks, schools, flats, telephone boxes, department stores — are often poorly understood.

The campaign to protect the best of architecture and design in Britain from 1914 onwards is at the heart of the Twentieth Century Society. Our staff propose buildings for listing, advise on restoration and help to find new uses for buildings threatened with demolition. Tragedies like the recent demolition of Modernist house Greenside, however, show how important it is to add your voice to the campaign.

Join the Twentieth Century Society, and not only will you help to protect these modern treasures, you will also gain an unrivalled insight into the groundbreaking architecture and design that helped to shape the century.

www.c20society.org.uk

Contents

Foreword   v

Acknowledgements   vii

Introduction   xi

1   Who Were McMorran & Whitby?   1

2   The Genesis of the Practice   5

3   Formative Years   11

4   Farquharson & McMorran and Post-war Britain   33

5   Passing the Flame   49

6   The Swinging Sixties   95

7   McMorran & Whitby's Legacy   123

List of Works   129

Obituary: Donald McMorran   141

Obituary: George Whitby   143

Assistants at 14 North Audley Street   145

McMorran & Whitby: Titles and positions held   146

'A Friendship'   147

Bibliography   148

Index   150

Picture Credits   154

Introduction

In 1907, Horace Farquharson (1874–1966), a young architect and former assistant to Sir Edwin Lutyens, took out a lease on an office building at 14 North Audley Street in the heart of London's Mayfair. This space was to become the base of one of Britain's most intriguing architectural practices of the 20th century, whose output remains shamefully unfamiliar and yet frequently appears, almost subliminally, in virtually every home in the country as it hovers in the background of televised broadcasts from outside London's Central Criminal Court. McMorran & Whitby's wonderfully weighty entrance, formed by those emblematic segmental-arched doorways, stands as an often-seen, but silent, witness to the way this practice has been treated by prevailing attitudes in architecture for over half a century. A full account of their story is given here at last.

The office at 14 North Audley Street produced work that was obscured by decades of dogmatism and indifference from an architectural community bedazzled by Modernism, but which was, as it turned out, ill-equipped to accomplish its utopian aspirations. It was unashamedly rooted in classical tradition when practically the entire architectural fraternity was looking the other way, but it was not traditional. In architectural terms, this course was, as E. Vincent Harris observed sympathetically some years later, the 'hard road'.[1] The work, because it refused to embrace blindly the dominant paradigm, was discredited by most, attracted the ire of some and was appreciated by few.

Given this historical backdrop, few practices were exposed to such overwhelmingly subjective critique. To understand the work that emanated from the architectural soap opera that characterised 14 North Audley Street, standing shoulder to shoulder with Gandy-Deering's fine late-Georgian St Mark's Church (1824–8), context is everything. To look just at the contemporary architectural press would be taking not only a singular and skewed perspective but also a very constrained one, since this work, especially latterly, was seldom published in the professional press or aired in the wider professional media. Eventually, having adopted a position of consistent censure, often hurtful but ultimately marketable, the architectural media began to censor the practice's work altogether. In a manner reminiscent of Stalinist-era practices, Farquharson, McMorran and Whitby gradually became 'non-persons'[2] in the eyes of the media and among many of their peers; this process of exclusion amounted to what McMorran and those on his side referred to as a 'dictatorship of taste'. The relatively early deaths of the two leading architects, Donald McMorran (1904–65) and George Whitby (1916–73), also ensured a swift and somewhat bitter end to what time now reveals was among the more enlightened, and certainly most enduring, architectural outputs in Britain since the 1920s.

Opposite: Entrance to the Central Criminal Court, Old Bailey, 1960–72

Now, as we are able to look back on this tumultuous period from the theoretical comfort of a new millennium, the works of architects like McMorran & Whitby are being appreciated, lauded even, for their enduring qualities, scholarly sophistication and endearing simplicity. These attributes are the very same ones that attracted so much vitriol when the buildings were designed, thus serving to effectively erase the diverse contributions of this practice from the collective consciousness of British architecture.

Time, and time alone, has a peculiar way of refining opinion, as tempers calm, emotions moderate, political will sways and, especially important to architecture, experience is gained – both by the architect and by the user. In the case of the work coming out of 14 North Audley Street, this experience was among the most acute in the country and the practical solutions that grew out of it have endured, and in many cases improved with time. The same cannot be said for many contemporary structures, whose visionary premise and theoretical vacuity have rendered them aged and, whether good or not, often stigmatised in the eyes of the user for their association with a period of architecture of which Britain can hardly be proud. More than a century after the original lease was taken out on these premises, the output of this office is at last being seen in new light and being appreciated for its quiet erudition and profound attention to detail. Only time could permit this reappraisal and, as more time passes, so this architecture will likely continue to improve its standing within the realm of 20th-century architecture in Britain.

Notes

1   Private correspondence from E. Vincent Harris to Donald McMorran; courtesy of the McMorran family archive.

2   Gavin Stamp, 'McMorran and Whitby, A Progressive Classicism', *Modern Painters*, 4:4 (Winter 1991), p59.

14 North Audley Street, Farquharson, McMorran & Whitby's office

1　Who Were McMorran & Whitby?

14 North Audley Street became the professional home of a great many committed architects with varied professional and cultural backgrounds. The practice's official title is therefore of far less importance than the professional family the firm came to represent, and whose evolution spans a large part of the 20th century. As is the case in all families, the complex interrelationships fuelled much rumour and intrigue among its members, and, inevitably, offered ample cause for joy and sorrow. We shall come to explore these as this story unfolds, but first it is necessary to establish the identities of the principal characters that provided the structure of this broad family tree.

The title McMorran & Whitby is perhaps something of a misnomer, as it derives from the surnames of the two partners heading this practice during its heyday, Donald Hanks McMorran and George Frederick Whitby.[1] Nevertheless, in name at least, it succeeded an earlier incarnation, Farquharson & McMorran, comprising Horace Cowley Nesham Farquharson and Donald McMorran, and for some time – to fit more comfortably within the taxman's steely embrace – it existed concurrently as Farquharson & McMorran and McMorran & Whitby and even, on occasions, collectively as Farquharson, McMorran & Whitby. Despite the changing names and shifting hierarchies within the firm, a true constant was the office at 14 North Audley Street.

At the head stood Horace Farquharson, a Victorian figure and the truest of gentlemen. Born in 1874 at Dundridge, Devon, Horace was the fourth of five sons among nine siblings. His father, Robert Farquharson, was a civil servant based in Calcutta and working as a postmaster and opium officer. Educated at Blundell's School, Farquharson was later articled to the firm of Gibson & Russell, before spending a year in the firm of Sir Edwin Lutyens, or the 'Great Lut' as he was to be later referred to fondly as in 14 North Audley Street. At the age of just 23, Farquharson established his own practice and gained considerable success in designing country residences. In 1907, at the age of 33, he became a Fellow of the Royal Institute of British Architects (FRIBA) and in the same year moved from 41 Montpelier Square, Kensington, to Audley Street, Mayfair, where he signed the lease with twins by the name of Coleridge.[2]

Arranged over five floors including a basement, the property offered considerable flexibility for sub-letting. This proved to be an inspired move and a considerable boon over the years, as the supply of work ebbed and flowed. Farquharson, the patriarch, remained actively involved with the machinations inside 14 North Audley Street until he died on 23 April 1966. His obituary in *The Times* echoes the warm sentiments and the highest regard that so many who knew him held for the man: 'Farquharson ought to have been born in the eighteenth century, but he contrived to bring much of its grace into our time.'[3]

Top left: Horace
Cowley Nesham
Farquharson

Top right: Horace
Farquharson (back
row second from
left) with his mother
and eight siblings

Bottom right: George
Whitby and his three
eldest children

Bottom left: Donald
McMorran

Next in line was Donald McMorran, an erudite and strong-willed architectural fundamentalist. He was born in Wallasey, on 3 May 1904, to William Edwin McMorran and Edith (née Hanks). His family soon returned to their native north-west London, where he attended Harrow County Grammar School. While McMorran was still at school, a neighbour introduced him to Farquharson, whom he went to work for in January 1921. In 1925, at the age of 21, he was awarded an RIBA Pugin Travelling Studentship, following which he worked for a short period with Percy Morley Horder (1870–1944). From May 1926 to 1935, McMorran was an assistant to Emanuel Vincent Harris (1876–1971), under whom he gained valuable experience and established a number of important professional relationships. It was while working with Harris in December 1930 that McMorran passed his Architectural Examination, becoming an Associate of the RIBA (ARIBA) in April the following year.

In 1935, McMorran left Harris to reunite with Farquharson, this time not as a student but as a partner – and so the firm Farquharson & McMorran was born. For a man who professed to despise the Establishment, McMorran amassed a formidable arsenal of letters after his name, becoming an FRIBA in 1943, an ARA in 1955, an FSA in 1956 and a full Royal Academician in 1962. By the time McMorran died on 6 August 1965, aged 61, his forthright attitude had earned him respect and reprobation in equal measure. This is reflected in the thinly veiled critical tone used in his obituary in *The Times*, in which his 'traditional beliefs' and 'sympathies' were misunderstood as being 'those of an earlier generation'.[4] The failure of the writer (probably the critic J. M. Richards) to rein in his own opinions drew criticism from various quarters, including a letter from W. A. Eden which *The Times* printed four days later, though it chose not to publish a letter from John Betjeman defending his friend and opposing the newspaper's 'introduction of prejudice' into the writing of their obituaries.[5] It could be said that McMorran brought it upon himself, for he was a man who, in life as much as in death, divided opinion.

Succeeding McMorran at the helm at 14 North Audley Street was George Whitby, a vivacious character with a generous spirit. Born on 17 August 1916 to Cyril Whitby and Mabel (née Jennings), he was one of four children and attended Ealing Grammar School from where he went on to study architecture at Regent Street Polytechnic. Throughout his years as a student, he worked during the day as an assistant for Welch, Cachemaille-Day & Lander and later with Farquharson & McMorran, while studying at night. At the outbreak of the Second World War he volunteered his services to the Royal Engineers and served at Dunkirk before being stationed in North Africa and the Middle East, where he was able to find time at least partially to satisfy his interest in architecture by studying sites in Egypt, Palestine, Transjordan, Syria and Lebanon.[6] Whitby's service in assembling Bailey bridges in the deserts of North Africa earned him a military MBE, but he was then wounded in action and spent two years in hospital. After the war, he returned to Britain to pursue his architectural career, and passed his Architectural Examination in December 1946 before becoming an ARIBA in 1947 and an FRIBA in 1954. After the war, he became a partner in the firm of Walters & Kerr-Bate. In 1958, he moved back to 14 North Audley Street and worked again with Farquharson & McMorran before becoming a partner during their most prolific period. Whitby died, at the age of 56, on 22 February 1973, by which time the original spirit and fundamental ethos of the firm had already passed away, though the practice continued in name until the early 1980s.

Notes

1   This partnership was not even a legal entity until McMorran, on his deathbed, insisted that both partners sign the partnership documents.

2   What happened to these two is not known, but Farquharson ended up owning the entire lease.

3   *The Times*, 3 May 1966.

4   *The Times*, 10 August 1965.

5   *The Times*, 7 May 1966.

6   RIBA Nomination Paper notes.

2   The Genesis of the Practice

The evolution of McMorran & Whitby reaches back well before the few short years from the late 1950s to the mid-1960s when these two eminent architects enjoyed their successful partnership. To understand fully the ideals and aspirations of the practice, it is necessary to begin with the work of Farquharson in the early 20th century and the fanatical enthusiasm with which McMorran, as a student 'who must have dreamed architecturally',[1] absorbed everything he could of the discipline.

This crucial period led ultimately to the establishment of the firm Farquharson & McMorran, which in turn gave the young Whitby the experience during his student years that was needed when he later assumed the vital role of partner. When the lens of architectural history is widened to accommodate these formative years, it is not surprising to see how, after the Second World War, McMorran & Whitby were able to 'keep their heads while all around them were losing theirs'. Indeed, this was noted by Charles Holden, one of the universally acclaimed masters of 20th-century architecture in Britain and a man McMorran admired deeply, who wrote: 'I am glad to know that you have kept a level head in all this welter in search of novelty of expression in architecture, for I always found your designs very satisfying.'[2] How sad it is, however, that their method was so misunderstood by most of their contemporaries, and that they never lived to enjoy the time when the enduring and endearing character of their work would vindicate their learned approach.

Horace Farquharson

Horace Farquharson was among the last in a long line of British architects 'whose chief concern was the English country house'.[3] The subject and building type suited his Victorian demeanour, and although he did not spend long in the office of Sir Edwin Lutyens he would have gained inestimable experience and confidence in this particular realm of architecture from his time under the watchful eye of such a master. His work included original designs, such as at Bailiff's Cottage, Salisbury; East Lymden, Wadhurst; Hele Manor, Dulverton; Lodge Hill, Farnham; Fairoak, Wokingham; and Linholme, near Dorking; as well as restorations or adaptations, such as at Castle Martyr, County Cork; Pilgrims Hall, Brentwood; Send Manor, Surrey; Sharpcliffe Hall, Staffordshire; the manor at Adhurst St Mary, Petersfield; The Lowe, Wellesbourne, Warwick; and Woolston Grange, Somerset; and with Norman Evill, who may also have worked for Lutyens, he also designed additions to a house at Holmbury St Mary, Dorking.

Opposite: Ventilation outlet on the roof of the City of London Police headquarters, Wood Street, with buildings by Norman Foster (left) and Richard Rogers (right) in the background

Donald McMorran

It was into this professional environment that McMorran entered in 1921, at the age of just 16. He was young enough to have escaped the horrors of the First World War but old enough to appreciate the critically altered world it precipitated; McMorran was fascinated by progress, and was especially drawn to the idea of flight. Many of his early sketches were of biplanes, and he would create scale models meticulously carved in wood, whose perfectly formed propellers would spin round furiously on their axles of metal pins at the slightest hint of a breeze. However, colour-blindness brought a swift end to any aspirations McMorran had of a career in the aeronautical industry, and so he concentrated his efforts on his other love: architecture.

Few words can describe the passion with which the young McMorran set about learning his chosen trade. For this, McMorran owed a debt to his art teacher, George Neal, who encouraged him to make black-and-white sketches of buildings. He was one of a group of young boys that would go out on trips with a senior student, Hugh Braun (later FSA and ARIBA), to sketch the churches of Middlesex. His early sketchbooks demonstrate an evident talent in drawing architectural detail almost to the point of pedantic obsession, and a determination to understand how buildings are put together in stone. The approach, though palpably raw in its early stages, is still impressive in its scope.

As his talent materialised, it was vital that McMorran gained the professional experience he needed to apply this talent. Farquharson recognised McMorran's 'persistent and extraordinary avidity for architecture'[4] and provided him with the break he required to learn the practicalities of a life in architecture. With typical aplomb, having been given Farquharson's address on 7 January 1921, McMorran wrote to him and was interviewed five days later. With Farquharson admitting that his work showed 'very distinct promise',[5] McMorran was working in the office the following week. A month later, he began his evening classes at Regent Street Polytechnic and for the next five years concentrated on his studies, sketching and gaining professional experience. It was during this time that one of the draughtsmen in Farquharson's office saw McMorran's 'excellent architectural sketches' and suggested that he enter for the RIBA Pugin Travelling Studentship. In 1923 his application was unsuccessful, but in 1924 he won.

At the end of his second year at the Polytechnic, he was awarded a Second Year Medal and a couple of months later bought a second-hand bicycle. This vehicle thereafter took him around much of Britain on his numerous 'expeditions' and gave him an education in architecture and architectural history that no school could have provided. McMorran's expeditions were of a professional and a recreational nature, ingredients which were blurred throughout his life: many years later he likened his first introduction to a foreman, 'the man who is going to help my job into the world', to the schoolmaster 'who is to do the same for my child'.[6]

McMorran's close friends or family members often joined him on his cycle tours, but it would invariably be his beloved sister Peggy (through whom he later met his wife,

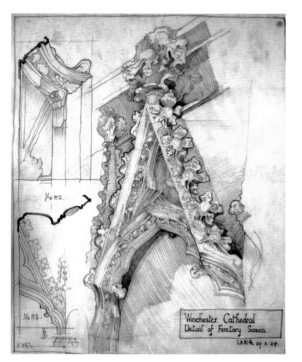

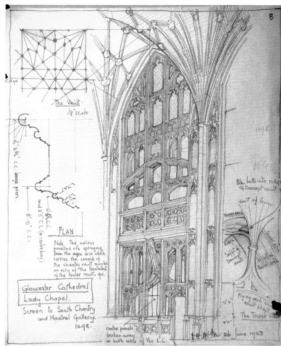

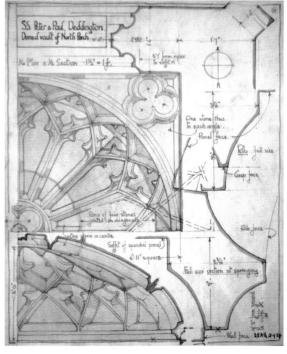

Drawings made by McMorran during numerous expeditions

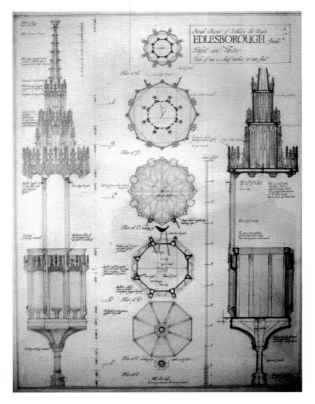
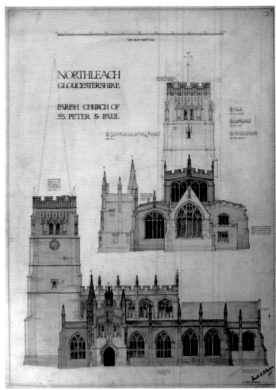

Pulpit at Edlesborough and measured drawing of St Peter's, Northleach

Margaret Cox) or his closest friend from his school days, Stanley Tempest, who proved the most reliable touring partners. Within a year, McMorran had cycled over 1,000 miles on tours of Kent, Gloucestershire and Northamptonshire. In the three months from late April to early August 1924, he covered a further 1,000 miles, during which he measured Lowick Tower and the pulpit at Edlesborough. These two expeditions cost him a replacement back tyre and new inner-tube but won him the Pugin Travelling Studentship, which he received on 19 January 1925. His measured drawings of St Peter's Lowick and the pulpit at Edlesborough were published in the *Builder* in January of the same year. This would be the first of many published works to appear in the *Builder* throughout McMorran's career, when it came to be the only professional journal consistently willing to feature his work.

One month after completing expeditions around Oxfordshire in April 1925, and with 3,200 miles behind him, McMorran set off on his Pugin Tour with Stanley Tempest. McMorran chose to travel around Northumberland and southern Scotland, researching and documenting the region's architecture because it had 'not previously been visited by a Pugin student'.[7] His key interests were Hexham Abbey, whose 'beauty and interest' he felt 'would be hard to exaggerate', and Warkworth Castle, as well as military buildings from the Border Wars.

The tour clearly made a significant impact on McMorran. Despite his relatively young age of 21, it is from his ability to compare structures and his appreciation of architectural detail that one gets a sense of his keen eye and genuine affection for the subject. His pioneering, if naive, enthusiasm is infectious. He genuinely felt that he 'was breaking fresh ground from the architectural point of view' and by the end of the tour, after making 22 measured drawings and 51 sketches, he reflected warmly: 'all circumstances combined to provide an experience to which I shall always look back with the greatest of pleasure'.

Notes

1   McMorran's Reference Letter by Farquharson, 4 February 1931; courtesy of the McMorran family archive

2   Letter from Charles Holden to McMorran, 28 August 1955; courtesy of the McMorran family archive. Holden added 'I have done a little exploring myself in my time and I can sympathise with the desire for novelty and for breaking new ground – but not at the expense of a clear expression of function and the logic of structure and purpose'.

3   *The Times*, 3 May 1966.

4   McMorran's Reference Letter by Farquharson, 4 February 1931; courtesy of the McMorran family archive.

5   ibid.

6   Donald McMorran, 'Everyday Things from the Architect's View Point', lecture, undated.

7   Donald McMorran, Pugin Report, 1925.

3 Formative Years

Early Professional Practice

One month before McMorran was awarded the Pugin Travelling Studentship, he had won a Bronze Medal at Regent Street Polytechnic for his design for a music pavilion. These successes in academia marked a period in McMorran's earlier career in which he was starting to make a name for himself.

The first months of 1925 saw McMorran submit one of 477 entries for a competition by *Country Life* to design a residence in Moor Park, Hertfordshire. He was not short-listed. The panel of judges included Morley Horder and Sir Edwin Lutyens (though he was away in India at the time of the adjudication in March 1925). Soon afterwards, McMorran produced what was perhaps his first ever completed design – a doctor's residence, which was approved by the RIBA in May of that year. Later that summer, after

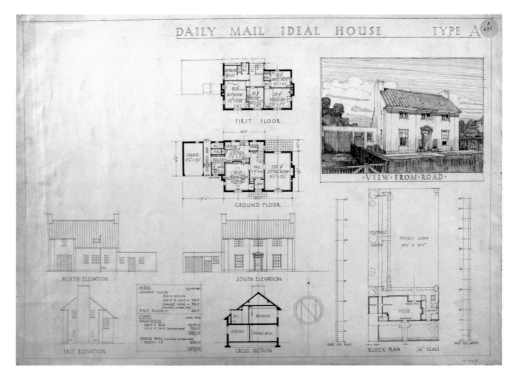

McMorran's submission to the *Daily Mail* Ideal Homes competition, 1927

Opposite: Entrance to the former Police Station and Section House, Greenwich, 1935–9

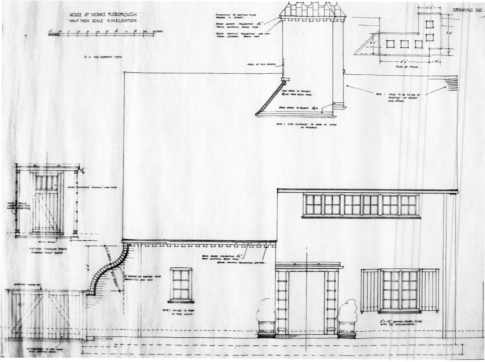

House at Monks Risborough for N.A. Richardson, 1930, original elevations and as built

his exhausting tour of Northumberland and southern Scotland, McMorran started to look for work as an architectural assistant. In August, he was interviewed by a member of staff at Lutyens's office, but nothing came of it. A fortnight later he was accepted by Morley Horder. Both would have seen his work for the *Country Life* competition a few months earlier.

By early 1926, McMorran was again submitting entries to competitions in the hope of finding work and of making a name for himself. This process was given a boost by his Pugin Studentship drawings being publicly exhibited for two months at the RIBA. At the same time, he submitted competition entries for projects in Blackpool and Topsham, and designed a house for his uncle Alec, followed two months later by working drawings for a house for a Mr Bowd. In 1927, he achieved considerable success in the *Daily Mail* Ideal Homes competition, receiving a Second Premium for his design of a 'Class A' house (valued at £1,500) and a Third Premium for a 'Class B' house (valued at £850). McMorran had the chance to build his first house in 1930, at Monks Risborough, Buckinghamshire, where his design reflects Lutyens's influence in the steep roofline and massive chimney, and Voysey's in the discrete strip of windows above the porch.

In the Shadow of the Smallest of Giants

On 17 May 1926, and just three weeks after passing his final RIBA examination,[1] McMorran left Morley Horder to work as an assistant for the prolific and successful, if somewhat unfairly maligned, architect, E. Vincent Harris, who 'was prepared to engage him for £5 per week'.[2] Born in Devonport in 1876 and educated at Kingsbridge Grammar School, Emanuel Vincent Harris (OBE, RA, FRIBA) 'sallied forth from his beautiful but sleepy county to raid, if not always conquer, new worlds'.[3] Articled to the Plymouth architect James Harvey, Harris subsequently travelled to London to work for Edward Keynes Purchase for six months and to study at the Royal Academy Schools, followed by a year as assistant to a former Pugin Scholar, Leonard Stokes (1858–1925), then three years with the former RIBA President, Sir William Emerson (1843–1924). Harris then spent seven years at the London County Council during 'the halcyon days of the LCC's architecture department'.[4] Like so many young and ambitious architects, Harris sought a way into private practice through competitions, which he entered frequently. His first taste of success came when he was still in his twenties. He was awarded second place in a competition to design a town hall at Torquay. In 1908 Harris won a competition for Mid Glamorgan County Hall, completed in 1912, and embarked on private practice. He had several small triumphs before the First World War, followed by a string of disappointments. His next big break came in 1914, when he won a competition to design the new offices of the British Government's Board of Trade on the Embankment. This colossal development was to stand opposite the newly designed County Hall, for which Harris had unsuccessfully submitted designs in competition. The Board of Trade job was later

E. Vincent Harris, 1940s

abandoned, but Harris had made a sufficient name for himself to subsequently win several large projects that helped him to establish a sizeable independent office in St James's Square. 'One of his abilities was his shrewd assessment of his assistants, among whom numbered several who afterwards achieved distinctions', including John Watson, Arthur Bailey, Tom Mitchell, Frank Hodge and Marshall Clifton.[5] The office specialised in public buildings, particularly town halls, for Harris 'apparently was being offered them up and down the country, almost as if they were multiple shops and he the architect to the firm'.[6] Many years later, he would return to the government project on the Embankment, and today the huge office housing the Ministry of Defence stands as one of his principal works.

In 1951, the year that the Festival of Britain brought modern architecture centre stage, Harris received the Royal Gold Medal. He was aptly described by one of his longest-serving assistants, Arthur Bailey, as the 'smallest of giants',[7] but Harris's short stature belied a formidable personality. The tone and brevity of his acceptance speech at the RIBA for the Royal Gold Medal was typical of the man and reflected precisely what he thought of the age he found himself living in. McMorran frequently declared his professional debt to Harris, but this speech was something even the notoriously obdurate McMorran would find hard to emulate. As Harris scrambled on to the rostrum to address the great and the good in British architecture, he said simply: 'Look,

Harris's assistants on the roof of Manchester Library (left to right) Arthur Bailey, John Watson, Tom Mitchell, Marshall Clifton, unknown, Frank Hodge, Donald McMorran

a lot of you people here tonight don't like what I do and I don't like what a lot of you do but I am proud and honoured to receive the Royal Gold Medal.'[8]

McMorran gained considerable experience as an assistant to Harris, working as job architect on the design for Manchester Library and Town Hall extension, won in 1927 and completed in 1938. This project presented McMorran with the opportunity of working on a circular plan – a form he kept returning to throughout his career, but which ultimately eluded him as an independent practitioner.

Just as Harris broke free of salaried employment in a public office through competitions, so he let his assistants attempt the same, encouraging McMorran 'to spend all [his] spare time on public architectural competitions',[9] an opportunity which McMorran and his friend and colleague, Arthur Bailey, accepted enthusiastically. Both individually and, often, together they had some degree of success. In 1927, McMorran was awarded Second Premium for his proposal for the University of Western Australia, Perth, with an eclectic design that was neither Tuscan nor Gothic but possessed shades of both. Over the next few years, he and Bailey were awarded a string of second premiums for their proposals for Wimbledon Municipal Offices and Assembly Hall (1927–8); Wyggeston Grammar School, Leicester (1928); Ellesmere Port and Whitby Urban District Council Municipal Buildings and Market Hall (1929);[10] municipal office buildings in the City of Bradford (1929); Swansea Civic Buildings (1930); and

McMorran at his drawing board with a plan of
Manchester Library in the background,
late 1930s

Wolverhampton Assembly Halls (1934). For Wolverhampton, McMorran and Bailey
were able to share a £250 prize and upon hearing the news McMorran celebrated by
taking the two loves in his life at that time, his sister Peggy and his girlfriend Margaret
Cox, to tea, followed by a performance of *King Lear*.

The earlier designs for Leicester and Swansea were very different in scale and detail,
but both were more explicitly classical than anything McMorran would eventually
build. The design for Wolverhampton, however, shows a maturity and growing confidence in simple detailing and massing of broad screens of unadorned surfaces in brick
and stone. McMorran and Bailey's design houses two large public halls, one seating
2,000 and the other seating 800. Both are contained in a single block occupying the
whole site, but clearly display the two elements' independence from one another
through the subtle use of surface detailing and arrangement of individual elements.
The principal devices that unite the entire composition are the roofline and the rusticated band encircling the building. There are hints of McMorran's later work here: the
unifying roofline, the round arches, and the expanses of brickwork.

However, while these competitions demonstrate a steady development of
McMorran's style and experience, it was an entirely different type of project for which
he would gain a degree of recognition while working for Harris. It was also one that
appealed to his aeronautical sensibilities. In 1928, McMorran prepared plans for a
student competition for 'London's Future Airport' organised by the Gloster Aircraft
Company and the RIBA. The winning design was expected to meet the demands of
London's airline industry in 1943, 15 years hence. The brief was to design an airport
with a capacity of 300 aircraft, a first-class hotel accommodating 200 persons, offices,

garages and a direct Underground line to central London from the hypothetical site on Mitcham Common in south London.

In preparing for the competition, the students were given plans and drawings of the then-new Croydon Airport and Berlin's Tempelhof Airport. McMorran's design, despite demonstrating obvious shortcomings in tackling the issue of circulation of aircraft on the ground, was considered to be 'the best piece of general composition' and the judging panel awarded the £125 first prize jointly to him and Mark Hartland Thomas. Among the eight esteemed judges were Sir Edwin Lutyens, Charles Cowles-Voysey and E. Vincent Harris. In their concluding comments, the judges felt the final designs failed to show any 'sufficiency of vital imagination' and all contained obvious faults. The 'flashes of imaginative genius' that Le Corbusier had demonstrated in his proposals for an airport in his scheme for *Urbanisme* caused the British architectural press to be 'reconciled to the comparative mediocrity of the designs at the r.i.b.a.'.[11]

Among the most conspicuous aspects of McMorran's design is the arrangement of the overall scheme, and in particular the large circular 'field' which derives from McMorran's decision to ensure that aircraft could take off and land in any direction, thereby offering a runway of equal length in any orientation. On this basis, the circulation of aircraft from and to the field – via refuelling stations, conveyor belts and passenger arrival and departure points – gave this design its geometric and somehow rational layout.

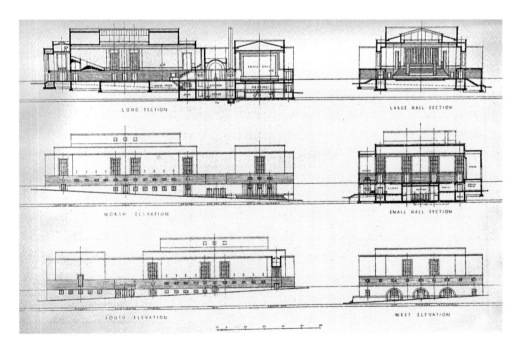

McMorran & Bailey's design for Wolverhampton Civic Centre, 1934

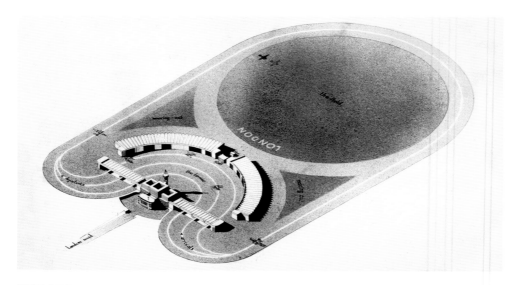

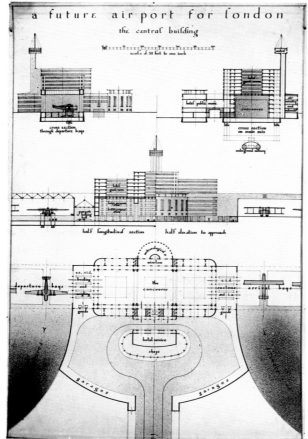

McMorran's proposal for London Airport, 1928

The two airport buildings were laid out in a D-shaped plan and comprised hangars and accommodation for pilots and mechanics in the semicircular section and, detached from this, the main terminal building. This was arranged around a symmetrical plan with the control tower in the centre and two wings under which the aircraft passed in the course of refuelling and collecting or dropping off passengers. In designing the main terminal building, which contained a hotel, McMorran employed the defensive planning of internal courtyards to protect the guest bedrooms from aircraft noise, a solution that McMorran would revisit throughout his career – to a certain extent out of utility but also because he was a great admirer of the Italian piazza, partly for the uniquely gratifying space it creates and partly for the positive effect it has on the ambience of the buildings surrounding it.

Whatever might be concluded from McMorran's winning design, it earned him a degree of publicity in Germany following its publication in *Neuzeitlicher Verkehrsbau*, in which he appears alongside eminent modernists such as Erich Mendelsohn and Ludwig Mies van der Rohe, an apparently curious irony for the man whom the Modern Movement in post-war Britain was to cast as their arch-enemy. However, even as far back as 1931 McMorran would have enjoyed the ostensible paradox, knowing it not to be so.

It was while working in Harris's office that McMorran prepared designs for what would be his real professional breakthrough. In early 1935, McMorran submitted plans for a competition to design the new municipal offices and a clinic in the historic heart of York. He won on 2 December 1935 and received a £250 award. The site was that of the old prison, and was hemmed in by the River Fosse to the east, Clifford's Tower to the west and 'an architectural group of the greatest interest' within the castle walls to the south. Owing to the historical importance of the site it was deemed 'essential that the new buildings shall also form a definite contribution to the effect of this group'.[12]

McMorran's proposal incorporated the existing female prison as one wing of a larger symmetrical unit, with the clinic comprising the central portion and the new offices forming the adjacent wing. The three elements were connected by screen walls. Punctuating these screens were four openings that, for the first time in McMorran's work, were capped with what became his characteristic segmental arch. The screen, too, was a device that he returned to in his later work, especially in his larger housing schemes and municipal projects. To unite the entire elevation of the project, McMorran continued a rusticated band that spanned the length of both new buildings, from the classical façade of the female prison, through the clinic and to the municipal offices. Further reinforcing this sense of unity among the three elements was the landscaping, comprising grassed areas planted with trees in the centre of a double carriageway in front of the buildings.

The three-storey offices were designed in a restrained classical style with monumental pretensions. As with his design for Wolverhampton, McMorran's symmetrical configuration employs a combination of rusticated stonework and brick, tall windows and subtle detailing in the brick surfaces to emphasise different elements of the building. Dominating the façade is the central tower, which, in order to accen-

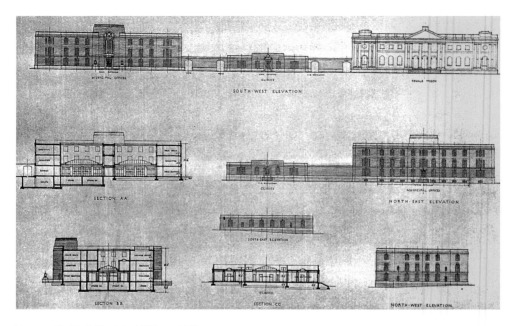

Proposal for York Municipal Offices, 1935

Resubmitted proposal after the Second World War

tuate its elevation, breaks through the entablature and is given lightness through the huge window that spans two full floors. Complicating the issue slightly was the fact that the building had to be designed so that it could be constructed in two phases. This meant that although the foundations and basement for the entire scheme had to be laid, only one portion of the office building would be constructed initially, with the rest following at a later date. Sadly for McMorran, the foundations were all that were constructed, since the Second World War caused the project to be abandoned, and although he resubmitted a somewhat retrograde design after the war the project was never rekindled.

The eight years with Harris had given McMorran the necessary experience to go out into the architectural world on his own and on equal terms with his former mentors. Shortly before leaving Harris's office on 12 October 1935 to rejoin Farquharson at 14 North Audley Street, McMorran had designed Harris's home in Fitzroy Park off Hampstead Heath in London. McMorran always maintained that an architect should never design his own house because the discipline inherent in the relationship with the client was essential and so one might assume that view was therefore shared by Harris. His departure from Harris's office might have marked the end of a professional relationship, but the two men remained close friends and allies throughout their lives, with Harris even making a marriage proposal to McMorran's widow in 1965, the same year his own wife, Edith, died.

Piles and foundations being prepared for York Municipal Offices

E. Vincent Harris's home at 10 Fitzroy Park, Highgate, 1932–4

Farquharson & McMorran

On 10 October 1935, McMorran wrote to Farquharson expressing 'how deeply [he] appreciated the privilege of being associated' with him. His excitement and gratitude were obviously profound, since he went on to say: 'The sudden change in my immediate prospects makes it difficult to express what I feel.'[13] Four days later McMorran arrived for work at North Audley Street, bringing 'a breath of fresh air into the office'.[14] Many years later Farquharson's secretary, Hilda Smith, remarked on his kindness and helpfulness, as well as his 'great love for his mother and sister'.[15] This move marked the formation of the nucleus of the practice that would later evolve into McMorran & Whitby. Although nobody had any way of knowing it at the time, the subsequent arrival of George Whitby at 14 North Audley Street as an 18-year-old assistant while undertaking his studies in architecture at Regent Street Polytechnic was to be the start of a professional liaison that would last the rest of their lives. However, between then and the mid-1960s, when the practice reached its prolific acme, the world would again go to war and Britain's architectural community would be transformed in the fallout. Before the war, the nascent partnership of Farquharson & McMorran enjoyed considerable success, designing in the space of a couple of years two of their most renowned buildings: a police station in Hammersmith and a police station and section house in Greenwich.

Before these two successes, Farquharson & McMorran narrowly missed the opportunity to design a new police station in London's St Marylebone, coming third in an

Elevation of Marylebone Police Station, 1937, unbuilt

Hammersmith Police Station, 1938–9

open competition assessed by the Metropolitan Police's in-house architect George Mackenzie Trench, against whom McMorran later competed successfully for Devon County Hall. What the assessor termed a 'severely academic mould',[16] from which Farquharson & McMorran's proposal for Marylebone Police Station emerged, provides a clear foretaste of things to come. The four-storey structure anticipates much of what can be found in McMorran's later work: the rusticated base, careful arrangement of the fenestration and attention to detail in the size and dimensions of the openings, the shallow-pitched roof and the prominent chimney stacks. Like so much of McMorran's output, the proposed design was a consequence of countless painstaking hours calculating the correct arrangement of the elevation so that each element was perfectly in proportion with every other and in its relation to the whole – a visual symphony in stone and brick. However, the somewhat dumpy design for Marylebone suggests this approach required a little honing yet, as the main body of the building, flanked by wings, provides more a sense of corpulence than composure. Pierce was critical of the design for failing to 'build up as a mass from all points of view'.[17] Despite losing out to Vine & Vine and Sir John Burnet, Tait & Lorne, Farquharson & McMorran's efforts were not wasted, as they would very shortly have the opportunity to use the elements of this design as the basis for the new police station in Hammersmith.

Hammersmith in many respects is a more refined and accomplished version of the scheme for Marylebone. McMorran's work can be seen to have evolved and matured, and elements of the design would reverberate through virtually every one of his later buildings. The elevation, unmistakably derived from the Italian Renaissance tradition, presents a dignified and humane air, giving the building an 'atmosphere of friendliness'.[18] Symmetrically composed, the façade is classically arranged into three portions: the base, middle and top. These Farquharson & McMorran sought to distinguish clearly by using Cornish-granite facings (traditional to London police stations) to create a ground-floor plinth, with buff London bricks on the two upper floors. The top is set apart by a shallow-pitched roof, firmly anchored in the centre by a bold brick chimney stack, very much derived from Lutyens via Harris, and itself divided into three elements arranged horizontally by the use of different materials. Above all, however, Hammersmith illustrates McMorran's admiration for the proportional systems employed by classical architects. At Hammersmith he used the double square to determine the arrangement of all the elements on the façade, including the mannered non-alignment of windows on the top floor with the bays below. Although such rules are assumed to be classical, it did not stop Le Corbusier from applying them in some of his works. McMorran had special $\sqrt{2}$ set squares manufactured for this specific purpose, and it can be observed in many of his subsequent façades. The consequence of the composition being so completely calculated is breathtaking, for as H. S. Goodhart-Rendel (1887–1959) said of its façade, it is 'aesthetically nearly perfect. I believe it to be the best thing of its kind in London'.[19] This 'exquisite police station' was noted by one obituarist as 'the best building that never got a London Architecture Medal'.[20]

It is clear that the detailing and the positioning of the elements on the elevation have been thoroughly considered and help to reflect the functions of the spaces within. The ground floor, faced in granite, contains largely public or semi-public areas, including the reception, waiting rooms and general office. The first floor possesses the largest windows, set in granite surrounds and decorated only by shallow cornices supported on simple consoles. Their formal appearance befits the function of the private offices behind, as does the more domestic character of the diminutive windows on the second floor, which serve the officers' private accommodation. A sense of proportion has been worked into the design through the insertion of recessed sections above the windows on the top floor, as well as beneath the windows on

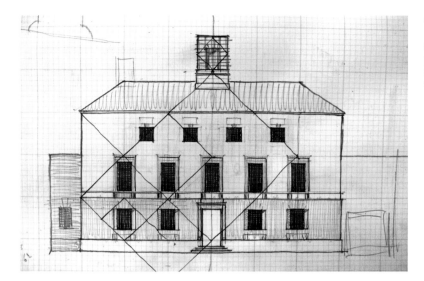

Sketch by McMorran showing the proportional relationships of the façade, 1938

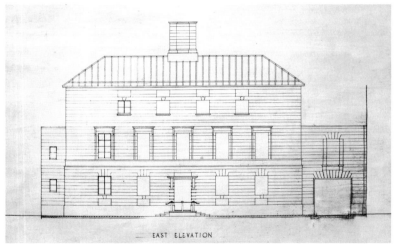

EAST ELEVATION

Sketch by McMorran of the final version of the façade, 1938

the ground floor – here hinting only that there might be a basement below. Despite the fact that this detail might give the windows the 'uncomfortable impression of having slipped down in their openings', the depression in the brick surface provides a measure of depth to an otherwise two-dimensional elevation, a device repeated again in the detailing of the chimney.[21]

Behind the façade, the entire site extends approximately 60 metres west to the railway tracks of the London Underground. The main building has a depth of approximately 40 metres, leaving space at the rear for garages and stables situated around a yard, access to which was provided by a private road along the northern boundary of the site. To conceal this entrance, the architects designed a large, square gateway, the

Former Greenwich Police Station and Section House, Blackheath Road, by Farquharson & McMorran, 1939

niche above which was deemed a 'trifle out of scale with the remainder of the treatment, but it is so intrinsically pleasant in design that the point is of no great significance'.[22] It is also curious to observe that while this building marks a critical stage in the development of McMorran's work, it also reveals the roots from which this work was drawn. The overall composition of the façade and the brick-and-silled niche above the gateway resonate strongly with previous works by Harris, most specifically his town hall at Braintree, Essex (commissioned by William Courtauld), and the screen and niche in London's Carlos Place respectively.[23] McMorran is said to have designed the latter with Harris in 1928 as part of an extraordinarily Italianate loggia and courtyard for Stephen Courtauld at the adjacent 47 Grosvenor Square.[24] Farquharson & McMorran deftly handled the large gateway at Hammersmith, the doors of which were originally made from solid teak, by composing it within a wing attached to the north of the main façade and by balancing this with another, narrower, wing on the south side. Both wings are set back slightly from the principal elevation, allowing it to retain its eminence within the overall composition and stand proud of the adjoining buildings.

The design of Hammersmith Police Station employs a structural concrete frame calculated to withstand the collapse of the superstructure in the event of an air raid, thus rendering the basement available as an official shelter. Fortunately, it survived the war and in 1955 was praised for being 'the finest small building put up in London in the past 20 years'.[25] In an assessment of four contemporary police-station designs published in the *Builder* in 1942, Julian Leathart claimed it to be 'by far the best of the collection', since it was the 'only design which is governed by a sustained sensitiveness of purpose'.[26] He went on to write:

> *I find the patterning of the two dimensional elevation altogether delightful, the horizontal lines' balance is as skilfully contrived and pleasing as the vertical division of window and wall. There is an almost archaic feeling in the treatment of the entrance doorway and the first floor window treatment which hints at Swedish derivatives. A similar treatment of console bracket [designed by Mr. G. Kruger Gray] can be seen on the small doorways at Dover House, Whitehall. Particularly elegant is the arrangement of the ground floor section: the entrance feature and steps, the placing of the flanking windows and the positions of the bracket lamps and coat-of-arms, set on a field of plain ashlar walling, produce one of the most successful compositions I have seen for a long time. I like, too, the change from the five-range principal windows to the four-range above.[27]*

It is said that Whitby, as a student working for Farquharson & McMorran at the time, stood out in front of the police station on the opening night hoping for a policeman to come and ask him, 'What's in your bag, sir?' His answer would have been 'a brick', because he wanted to be the first to spend the night in the cells, but no officer presented him with such an opportunity.[28]

In 1990, Hammersmith Police Station was nominated for listing as 'one of Britain's most sophisticated police station designs'.[29] In several reports, it was noted for being 'the most important early work by the partnership',[30] but another contender for this accolade is an earlier work by Farquharson & McMorran. The commission for a police station and section house for the Metropolitan Police on Blackheath Road, Greenwich, was the job that caused Farquharson to invite McMorran to join him in 1935 and earned the practice its first RIBA Medal. Farquharson, in his characteristically munificent manner, attributes the merits of this scheme to McMorran: 'Just when this job came into my office I was most fortunate in grafting on to my older stock an extremely able and energetic young branch. It is to this young branch that the whole of the credit both for the plan and for the design of this medal-winning building is really due. I refer to my partner, Donald McMorran.'[31]

In response, McMorran paid a debt of gratitude to his former master, Harris, 'without whose example and precepts this job would not have had the character' so admired by the judging panel.[32] Greenwich is not obviously a Harris-inspired solution, as Hammersmith Police Station so clearly is, but it possesses something outstanding. Sir Lancelot Keay, President of the RIBA when in 1946 the Greenwich building belatedly won a Bronze Medal, praised it as 'a piece of excellent planning', but also dared people to 'play with [it] … with some set-squares' to see 'why it is right, because of its perfect proportions'.[33] It is this level of analysis that will invariably reveal the rationale behind McMorran's elevations, as he refused to relent until completely satisfied that his elevations were proportionally true – causing him to labour endlessly at his drawing board, producing countless variations of the same elevation and each time meticulously measuring them out by hand from a blank sheet, much to the distress of his family at the weekend. 'The doting mother', McMorran once wrote, 'has nothing on an architect with a new design',[34] or as Harris once said to him: 'We both know there is only one thing that really matters, that is the work.'[35]

The Greenwich building was diplomatically described by Keay as being 'not too traditional to upset the Modernists and not too modern to upset the traditionalists'. The asymmetrical elevation was a departure for the architects, whose previous designs for public buildings were almost without exception symmetrical and often with at least a hint of classical detailing. Here, however, the design shuns such precedent and stands as a monument to simplicity fashioned in brick and hung on a concrete frame. The sweeping elevations of golden-brown brick penetrated by neat lines of rectangular windows with their tidy double sashes create an orderly, albeit faintly menacing, appearance that displays a remarkable sensitivity, particularly in the delicate use of Portland stone in the window surrounds and portico, above which sits the Royal Coat of Arms crafted by E. R. Broadbent. Ornament has been stripped right back in order to flaunt beautifully the expansive brick surfaces, with all their textural and visual qualities. The success of this effect relies on the quality of the finish. In his acceptance speech, Farquharson singled this out and praised the expertise of the builders, Messrs Galbraith Brothers Ltd, who, he said, 'turn out only one quality of craftsmanship, the best'. The façade is as sound today as it was when completed in 1939.

The building forms a series of volumes set back at intervals and standing on a wide base. As at Hammersmith, it attempts to express clearly the functions taking place within. The two functions of a police station and section house accommodating 120 bachelor officers are evidently defined, the former contained within the building's broad base on the ground floor, housing a gymnasium, games room, canteen, library, lounge, dining room and other services, while the upper floors, projecting six storeys from the longitudinal axis of the base, contain bedrooms, showers and lavatories. The internal corridor, accessing the bedrooms and services, forms the central axis of the symmetrical plan.

The police station and section house in Greenwich was the last building Farquharson & McMorran completed before the outbreak of the Second World War. However, during the few years that these two architects had been reunited much had happened in their private and professional lives that would determine the course of their practice once the war was over.

The Second World War

In the 1930s McMorran met Margaret, the daughter of the Sussex cricketer George Cox, through his sister Peggy who worked with her at St George's Hospital, Hyde Park Corner. There followed a courtship of two years that appeared to overwhelm McMorran, causing

McMorran and his wife Margaret (left) at an official opening

him to fill his diaries with mentions of his new-found love. In his letters to her, he revealed uncharacteristic tendencies: 'There *is* something Bohemian about me, I believe', he wrote shortly after rejoining Farquharson at 14 North Audley Street, when his relationship with Margaret remained a secret. Of their clandestine romance, McMorran wrote: 'I think it is partly because it is nice to pretend that nobody else knows – it is as though we are quite by ourselves, away from everybody and everything, and that would be lovely', but his secret was more a sign of his own uncertainty, which he freely admitted: 'I always dislike taking an important step … you know how I mistrust myself.'[36] He and Margaret were engaged in March 1936 and married the following year, on 30 April in Margaret's home village of Warnham, Sussex. A telegram was sent from the office which read 'all North Audleyites raise teesquares and typewriters to your binding health'. Nine months later a daughter, Susan, was born. In 1941 the McMorrans moved out of London to escape the bombing and settled into a handsome house in Dorking that would form the hub of their family for the rest of their lives.

Margaret was a loyal partner who stood by her husband through many vicissitudes and learned to bear his fanatical attitude to work. She was the keystone that held the family together, providing him the time and space to undertake his work and pontificate increasingly about the state of architecture, while devoting herself to bringing up their four children, Susan, Alexander, Eleanor and William. McMorran relied completely on the sanctuary, or 'home comforts' as he called it, that Margaret was able to provide. As he himself noted in a letter to her before they married: 'I love you, partly, because you have a way of looking serenely at the world. You may not <u>feel</u> serene, that will come in good time, but you look it, and that's a comfort.' Margaret was 'beautifully turned out'[37] and 'very elegant'[38] and a better person than McMorran could ever be. He knew it too, for he knew what he wanted from her, while having less to offer in return. 'Can you manage to go on looking serene, and loving with your body, and mothering, and being firm and kind to servants, and charming to customers, and tactful with relations, and careful with money, and looking beautiful, and egging me on, and ticking me off, and a hundred other things till death do us part?', he asked in one letter before they were married. He also asked, 'And what can I do in return except love you and try to earn as much as possible?' This was a relationship on his terms by a man attempting to cloak his professional ambition and personal insecurity in a virtuousness that deserved a place in the household. Without the 'strong-minded'[39] Margaret there would have been no successful architect or the domestic security he craved.

At the outbreak of war in 1939, the three men who had congregated at 14 North Audley Street were separated by the inevitable chaos. Architecture, and all its lofty aspirations to be the acme of human creative endeavour, was overshadowed by the forces of conflict and destruction. In the front line, figuratively and literally, was Whitby. He was injured in North Africa when a truck in which he was riding hit a landmine. Shreds of rubber from the tyres embedded themselves in his legs and thighs, giving him septicaemia and causing him to spend two years in a convalescent hospital in Jerusalem. He lived out the final stages of the war training troops in Wales for the impending assault on Japan. It was here, in May 1945, that Whitby met his future wife, Charmian Butler, who was a nurse with the Marines. The couple were married the following April.

Farquharson was far too old to be engaged in the fighting and McMorran was among that fortunate generation too young to be sent to the First World War and too old for the Second. The pair did a few small jobs during the war, including cottages at Westhumble, Surrey, and additions to a manor in Highworth, Wiltshire, for their friend and long-term client Raymond Cochrane, as well as winning a runners-up prize of £10 for an estate plan – one of a series of competitions to design war-time housing. However, between them their contribution to the war effort was two-fold. McMorran worked on the drawing team that designed the concrete casings for the top-secret Mulberry Harbour, the transportable harbour used during D-Day to offload men and supplies on to the Normandy beaches. He had to keep this assignment secret from his family, despite their pondering why he now used a different railway station at his home town of Dorking and travelled to Reading, not London. Earlier in the war, Farquharson and McMorran had joined the St Paul's Watch, a group committed to the defence of the City's great cathedral and the symbol of London's resistance to the Blitz. It was instrumental in preventing the destruction of St Paul's, putting out fires from incendiary bombs wherever they landed in the vicinity of the building.

After the devastation of the Blitz, in which the City and the East End had fared terribly, reconstruction was imperative. A high priority for central and local governments was the drafting and implementing of ambitious housing programmes. For Farquharson & McMorran, like many other architects at the time, these presented many opportunities. Amazingly, the projects they had completed before the war were all still standing, and the relationships they had built through these projects and the reputation they had made for themselves as architects of public buildings rendered them indispensable in a post-war Britain desperate to rebuild its shattered physical and administrative fabric.

Notes

1   This comprised, in 1925, the design and working drawings for the doctor's house, an airway Customs House and, in 1926, a shop front for a jeweller.
2   Letter from E. Vincent Harris to McMorran, 21 April 1926; courtesy of the McMorran family archive.
3   Prof. Charles Reilly, 'E. Vincent Harris', *Building*, September 1929, p393.
4   ibid., p394.
5   *Building*, 6 August 1971, p66.
6   C. H. Reilly, 'Expression in Municipal Architecture Today', *Building*, April 1931, p159.
7   Arthur Bailey, 'Mr Vincent Harris – Dedication to classical style', *The Times*, 13 August 1971.
8   ibid.
9   *Building*, 6 August 1971, p66.
10 For this scheme, he received only a commendation.
11 *Architect and Building News*, 1 February 1929, p166.
12 *Builder*, 6 December 1935, p1022.
13 Letter from McMorran to Farquharson, 10 October 1935; courtesy of the McMorran family archive.
14 Letter from Dorothy Groves to Margaret McMorran, 10 August 1965; courtesy of the McMorran family archive.
15 Letter from Hilda Smith to Margaret McMorran, 9 August 1965; courtesy of the McMorran family archive.
16 *Architect and Building News*, Supplement, 26 August 1938, p2.
17 ibid.
18 *Architect and Building News*, 29 March 1940, p303.
19 H. S. Goodhart-Rendel, 'Nightingales and Mud', in *Time and Tide*, 29 March 1947, p292.
20 *Builder*, 13 August 1965, p331.
21 Julian Leathart, *Builder*, 12 December 1942, p272.
22 ibid.
23 These have since been ruined by the additions of a doorway and windows in the niche and once-expansive brick surfaces.
24 For this information, I am indebted to Nick Holmes.

25 *Builder*, 29 April 1955, p698.
26 Julian Leathart, *Builder*, 12 December 1942, p271.
27 ibid., p272.
28 Clare Sims, interview with Charmian Smith (formerly Whitby), undated. Seven decades later any 'atmosphere of friendliness' this building once had appears to have vanished when its occupants officially cautioned McMorran's grandson under the Prevention of Terrorism Act for photographing their wonderful home.
29 Elain Harwood, unpublished report, 14 November 1990, H&F57, Historian's files, English Heritage. The police station was eventually listed on 28 September 1997.
30 ibid.
31 Horace Farquharson's acceptance speech on receiving the RIBA Bronze Medal at the awards for the best metropolitan building erected in the decade up to the end of 1946, quoted in *Builder*, 14 November 1947, p541.
32 Donald McMorran's comments on receiving the RIBA Bronze Medal at the awards for best metropolitan building erected in the decade up to the end of 1946, quoted in ibid.
33 Sir Lancelot Keay's comments on awarding the RIBA Bronze Medal for best metropolitan building erected in the decade up to the end of 1946 to Farquharson & McMorran, quoted in ibid.
34 Donald McMorran, 'Everyday Things from the Architect's View Point', lecture, *op. cit.*
35 Letter from E. Vincent Harris to McMorran, 20 August 1942; courtesy of the McMorran family archive.
36 Letter from McMorran to Cox, 8 December 1935; courtesy of the McMorran family archive.
37 Betty Murray, interview with the author, 4 September 2008.
38 Clare Sims, interview with Charmian Smith (formerly Whitby), *op. cit.*
39 ibid.

4 Farquharson & McMorran and Post-war Britain

In the autumn of 1940, large swathes of Britain's capital were devastated in the Blitz. Bombs fell indiscriminately, and on 9 September a large number of houses between Parkhill and Upper Park roads in Hampstead were destroyed in the first air raid on the borough. Such devastation had never before been witnessed in this salubrious corner of London, whose physical character is markedly genteel owing to its many 18th- and 19th-century houses. It comes as little surprise, then, to learn that when Hampstead Borough Council sought to rebuild on this site immediately after the war, they 'wished the scheme to have something of this traditional character',[1] and so the architect was asked to 'have regard to the character of the district, which was thought to suggest a building on traditional lines'.[2]

With their notable successes at Greenwich and Hammersmith – the latter, especially, classifying them among the architectural community as something of a traditionalist practice – Farquharson & McMorran appeared to be appropriate for the task. Although they had never designed large-scale domestic housing schemes, they had ample experience of country houses. Their work in Greenwich, with its 120 units for bachelor constables, however, was quite different from 92 dwellings for families and pensioners, with anything from one to six rooms, set on nearly a hectare (2½ acres) of land in a well-established residential area.

With Farquharson now well into his seventies, McMorran was unquestionably the more professionally active of the two partners and he was credited with the design of this project. It consisted of two identical, comparatively low-lying, terrace blocks lining the principal streets that enclosed the site. McMorran chose to face the main elevations of both buildings in a westerly direction, giving a more formal appearance to Upper Park Road to the west and allowing the 'rear' façade of the other block to face Parkhill Road to the east. However, the decorous design and characteristic attention to detail on both elevations ensured that neither vista was wanting or risked compromising the integrity of the streetscape on to which it faced. In fact, arranging each block in this manner ensured that the garden area between the two was not neglected in the way that communal spaces often are if overlooked only by the backs of the buildings surrounding the space. This open area was arranged as a garden, oriented in a north–south direction, and contained large trees that had survived the bombing, as well as minor access roads servicing the blocks.

Priority was placed on economy in the design and speed of construction, which

Opposite: Stone detail on the former Ede House, Police Section House, Hackney, London, 1950–1

Concept sketch by McMorran for Parkhill Road flats, Hampstead, 1946

started in February 1947 and was completed on St George's Day, 1949. Each block is built with a reinforced-concrete base and floors, with loadbearing walls; an element of standardisation meant that key components like windows and internal fittings could be prefabricated. LCC zoning regulations restricted the height of the buildings, which ranged from three to four storeys along the considerable length of each terrace. McMorran provided a rhythm to the roofline by stepping the elevations of the blocks, thus avoiding the monotony often characteristic of housing projects of this scale. This use of different heights reveals the careful planning inherent in the design. In effect, each block comprises three individual, yet conjoined, symmetrical units with diminutive wings. In the centre of each of these blocks, and at the two points at which they meet, is located an entrance into the building with a stairway serving the three-storey portions of the scheme and a lift serving the four-storey sections. Recessed balconies serving each kitchen are provided for each apartment, and arranged in vertical bands that give the façade a topology uncharacteristic of McMorran's work. However, other elements are conspicuously recognisable, including the careful arrangement and proportioning of the fenestration, the curvaceous door consoles, the shallow-pitched roof and the pair of broad chimney stacks. Here, as at Hammersmith, McMorran placed smaller windows on the uppermost level within recessed openings of brick that echo the size of the window openings on the lower floors.

A major element in this design was the attempt to conceal the pitched roof behind a parapet, as he had done at Harris's house on Fitzroy Park. This gives the blocks a distinctly more angular shape than at Hammersmith, where the eaves extending beyond the façade clearly define the separate elements of the elevation and the roof. From the side, McMorran has made little attempt to conceal these pitched roofs, which, when viewed tangentially, are made even more prominent by their bright white gables. He was clearly satisfied with this feature, as it reappears throughout his later work.

Each block accommodates 46 dwellings, containing 8 six-roomed flats, 14 four-roomed flats, 8 three-roomed flats and 16 two- and one-roomed 'flatlets' for the elderly – most of which have their own balcony and, in the four-storey sections of the building, are serviced by lifts. McMorran tried to ensure that all bedrooms faced east, and west-facing rooms were therefore kitchens and living rooms, which had been located next to each other to 'minimise labour and allow the easy supervision of children'.[3]

A conspicuous feature on the ground floor at the rear (east) of each block is the cloister, or 'undercroft', which gives on to stairs leading to the apartments, store rooms, laundry facilities and space to park prams and bicycles. The cloister itself was designed to provide comfortable access to the facilities on the ground floors as well as serving as a play area for young children. The fall of nearly five metres (16 feet) across the site from west to east is accommodated in the design by providing ground-floor access to the

The official opening of Council Housing, Parkhill Road, Hampstead, 1949, with McMorran (seated at right)

fronts (west) of each block and basement access to the rear (east). The names of the two buildings, Barn Field and Wood Field, are derived from the fields that once occupied the site.

Another significant housing scheme by Farquharson & McMorran was even more distant from the landmark public buildings normally associated with the firm. Wedged into the acute angle formed by the confluence of the busy East India Dock Road and Abbott Road in Poplar, a poor part of London's East End that had suffered terribly in the Blitz, was a housing scheme designed by Farquharson & McMorran for Poplar Metropolitan Borough Council. It comprised two blocks, Currie House and Dunkeld House, the former of which, at nine storeys, was comparatively high for the type of work these architects were accustomed to.

These two buildings were arranged in such a way as to provide a 'defensible space' in the centre of the site, shielded from the hostility of the environment around it created by the main roads. This protected space was created by the arrangement of both blocks, which were designed not to turn their backs on the outlying streets and spaces beyond the site. The result was a fair attempt to insert a large number of housing units on to a relatively unsympathetic site while providing a degree of sanctuary for the residents without excluding the neighbours. Sir Robert McAlpine & Sons were the general contractors for the two blocks, which were built using a concrete frame faced in brick. Construction in 1952–3 took just 17 months, reflecting the borough's urgent need to provide housing immediately after the war as well as the limited means which it had to achieve this. The frame was erected at a rate of one storey every fortnight owing to the high degree of standardisation in the design, which can be seen in the repetitive floor plans.

The buildings were very different from one another in form, although they both displayed evident economy. Dunkeld House, oriented in an east–west direction, was a series of low-rise three-storey blocks built of brick and designed to accommodate 18 five-person flats. Here the architects chose not to embellish the façades with any decorative features. The rectangular form was broken only on the north elevation, where the three entrances containing stairwells were set back from the façade and identified the four independent sections of the whole. Further defining this plan are small areas outside each of the four sections, delineated by a low wall. The south elevation was a sheer plane of brick with three rows of windows along its entire length and topped with chimney stacks, set in pairs but infilled to appear as a solid mass that concealed the water tanks on the roof. The hallways linking the street with the stairwells were housed under a segmental-arched ceiling – the first time since his design for York Municipal Offices that McMorran was able to use the form that was to become a signature motif.

Currie House, to the west of Dunkeld House and named after the founder of a large shipping company that had long associations with the area, was the principal building of the two. It was a huge block, 100 metres (330 feet) long and 30 metres (100 feet) tall, arranged in a sweeping arc. The architects sought to mitigate the impact of such a

Housing Estate, Parkhill Road, Hampstead, 1946–9

Currie House, 1952–4 (demolished August 2009)

Currie House (left) and Dunkheld House (demolished July 2009) (right) with McMorran's characteristic round-arch gateways defining internal public spaces

broad façade by using brick throughout, punctured by orderly lines of fenestration and white-painted communal balconies. The concrete surrounds, painted white, jarred a little against the rich brown brick, especially compared with the Portland stone that the architects were able to use on smaller projects with relatively larger budgets.

The building was another example of these architects' commitment to resolving the plan first rather than being constrained by facile matters concerning style. The result was a structure that was palpably modern, even displaying motifs and characteristics that might be regarded as belonging to the Modernist camp, such as the rounded, bull-nosed forms at each end of the building and the lean chimney stacks that pierced the roofline and rose dramatically skyward – evoking the tail fins of an aeroplane, and quite unlike the familiar solid chimney stacks that crown McMorran's other buildings. One device appearing for the first time on Currie House that would re-emerge on McMorran's later buildings was the round-arched gateway, marking the boundary of the site and helping to provide as well as define the defensible space within.

It was in the plan for Currie House that a claim to Modernism is best upheld. Economy was the driving force behind the design, in both space and cost. The block contained 86 dwellings, all of which were served by just two lifts and two stairwells. These gave access to a 'central gallery' that extended in an arc nearly the entire length of each floor along its centre, which in turn provided access to each flat. The central,

Plaque on Currie House proudly declaring the speed of construction in post-war Britain

One of the eight blocks of Fellows Road Estate, 1957

communal corridor was not only economical, but also dispensed with the need for external galleries, which the architects wanted to avoid since they can be unsightly and limit light to the flats behind. The flats were arranged in pairs, five pairs on each floor, separated by communal balconies with pre-cast concrete units spaced wide enough apart to allow children to see between them but not far enough to present a safety hazard. To prevent disturbance caused by noise that might emanate from the central gallery, the walls of all the flats were built using solid soundproofing brick set in lime mortar and the gallery floor slab was insulated from the main structure. Inside each flat was either a 'dining-kitchen' or a smaller 'working' kitchen, one or two bedrooms and a living room. The living rooms could be seen from the exterior, since they all had full-length windows offering maximum light and ventilation. The block also contained six maisonettes designed for six people. The flats were furnished with comparatively comfortable services, such as solid-fuel fires in the living rooms, with back boilers providing hot water, drying cupboards and space to store perambulators.

The constraints imposed by economy were evident, but the buildings, like so many of McMorran's, were constructed superbly. The once-confident Currie House bore two large stone plaques proudly displaying, like a badge of honour in the face of impossible adversity, the time it took to construct. However, despite their superb construction, after years of neglect and abandonment, in the summer of 2009 both buildings were demolished, the first of 14 North Audley Street's projects to be razed.

With a growing portfolio of public housing work, Farquharson & McMorran had the opportunity to return to Hampstead to design another housing estate shortly after

Currie House and Dunkeld House were completed. The site, being divided by Fellows Road and situated in a comparatively low-rise residential area, called for a smaller and more flexible design than Parkhill Road and East India Dock Road. The final design was in many ways a fusion of both their previous housing projects in a scaled-down form, displaying also elements of Hammersmith. The project is an interesting study of their work to date and although not among their most celebrated projects architecturally, it shows the direction in which the practice was heading.

The entire project comprises 8 three- and four-storey blocks: seven to the south of Fellows Road extending down to Adelaide Road, and one to the north, spanning virtually the entire width of the the the site. As with Parkhill Road, McMorran has arranged the blocks so that they all face in one direction, with all balconies facing north. Parkhill Road can be observed in the stepped outline of the larger block to the north of Fellows Road and in the relationship between the balconies and the fenestration on the buildings to the south. Interestingly, the balconies on the larger blocks have evolved to become communal walkways in order to provide access to the apartments from the exterior of the building, something the architects had tried hard to avoid at East India Dock Road. Nevertheless, Currie House is evoked in the slightly protruding, white concrete window surrounds; in the elongated openings for the living rooms; and, again, in the round-arched doorways, which this time provide entrance

Ede House, Hackney, 1950–1

directly into the building rather than serving as openings in screen walls to demarcate public space. The architects have taken, too, the shallow-pitched roof crowned with a prominent chimney stack from Hammersmith Police Station and used it on each of the blocks, the largest of which possesses two such features.

Another opportunity that came to Farquharson & McMorran immediately after the war owing to bomb damage was in Hackney, in East London. In 1938, as part of the Metropolitan Police's extensive rebuilding programme, a police section house serving the Borough of Hackney was substantially altered and redeveloped. The works included the demolition of the rear portion of the building, behind the newer and smaller façade facing Mare Street. The new portion was built using a steel frame and provided new accommodation for officers, while the portion containing the façade was converted from cubicle-type accommodation to separate individual bedrooms. However, two years after the completion of the works the building was hit by a bomb that landed precisely at the join between the two portions. The new rear section was relatively unharmed owing to its frame construction, but the front, built of loadbearing walls, suffered critical damage and had eventually to be demolished.

With their experience of Hammersmith Police Station for the same client, Farquharson & McMorran were ideally placed to take on this work, which they did under the direction of the Chief Architect of the Metropolitan Police, John Innes Elliott. The drawings of the new frontage were put on public display at the Royal Academy in early 1950, and the building was opened less than a year later on 26 February 1951 by the Foreign Secretary, James Chuter Ede. It provided hostel accommodation for 137 police officers. The new wing contained a uniform room on the lower ground floor, over which was a ground-floor canteen, recreational rooms on the first floor and individual bedroom accommodation on the top three levels.

This internal configuration is clearly expressed through the main elevation, which is classically arranged in its symmetry and in its composition of three parts. The base, faced in Portland stone as at Hammersmith, presents a stately appearance at street level, with four round-arched windows united by a string course running the width of the façade and arranged above semi-concealed openings that provide light and ventilation to the lower ground floor. The main entrance is situated in the centre of the façade and decorated lightly with a cornice supported by elongated consoles of a similar manner to those used at Hammersmith and Hampstead, at the base of which is McMorran's characteristic circle motif. Owing to the constricted nature of the site, especially where it meets the street, there are no ornamental steps leading to the main entrance, as occurs at Hammersmith. Instead, the steps are concealed immediately inside the main entrance.

Uniting the base with the central portion of the building are the surrounds of the tall windows serving the lounge and library on the first floor. The lines of fenestration at this point provide the connection between the formal aspect of the base and the less-fettered quality of the top three floors, characterised by their smaller windows set in slender surrounds. Shallow balconies divide the façade, interrupting its horizontal

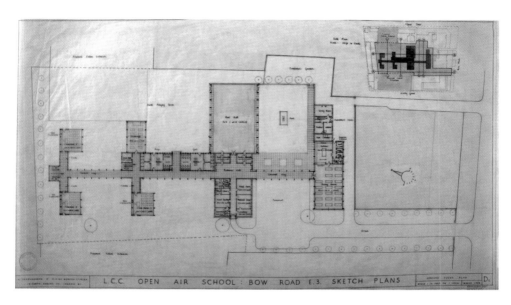

Sketch plans of Phoenix School, Bow Road, London, 1950–52

Phoenix School, Bow Road, London, 1950–52

lines and strengthening the vertical gestures that terminate in niches in the top portion of the building. The middle and top portions of the façade, which are faced in golden-brown brick, are clearly distinguished by a simple entablature composed of a slim architrave of Portland stone, an unadorned frieze in recessed brick and a delicate coping. Subtle detailing in the frieze brickwork, in the form of tiny notches, preserves the vertical relationship between the balconied windows and the niches below the crowning pediment.

The top of the building, perhaps owing to constraints imposed by the original structure behind, is treated quite differently from McMorran's other work. Although there are several familiar features, such as the hollow niches, recessed brickwork above the windows, and prominent chimney stacks, there is no space for a pitched roof parallel to the street. The composition, conversely, is perpendicular, resulting in a classical pediment that crowns the building – literally, as it happens, with the inclusion of a carved Metropolitan Police crest, placed in its centre.

The section house in Hackney marked the third prominent job for the Metropolitan Police by Farquharson & McMorran in little over a decade. Given the intervening war, it was a remarkable achievement, which helped to cement a relationship with the public sector that led to their most renowned work.

While the Hackney job was a development of earlier work for the Metropolitan Police, Farquharson & McMorran's school buildings marked a new approach to their architecture. The earliest of these was Phoenix School, or the 'Bow Road Open-Air School', for the LCC, and it led to larger commissions in the field later in the decade. It presented a unique opportunity. As with the jobs at Hampstead and Hackney and later at Battersea (see below), the site was 'created' by wartime damage. It was located on the busy Bow Road in East London, yet it was to provide over 180 'delicate' children with quiet and pleasant surroundings. Officially opened in September 1952, it was the first special school to be built since the war. *The Times* remarked that it was 'delight-fully designed with many novel features. Its six blocks of light and airy buildings are surrounded by lawns and trees … in its quadrangles; one gets an impression of almost rural quietude.'[4]

These open courtyards unite the whole very effectively and provide an area for horti-cultural activities to be undertaken by the children. To allow for this amount of outdoor space, the architects advised the school to build the classroom blocks two storeys high. Such a configuration was novel for an open-air school, which was normally arranged as single-storey classroom units accessed by open-sided corridors. However, at Bow Road, Farquharson & McMorran designed taller units interconnected by enclosed corridors, giving a greater sense of permanence. The covered corridors were built in brick and glass, and the junctions and stairwells were constructed from loadbearing brick, in which the familiar treatment of exposed brick and round arches reveals McMorran's hand. A similar treatment appears internally at Purford Green County Infants and Junior Schools, Harlow, which he and Farquharson designed shortly after Bow Road Open-Air School. Here, the classroom units were assembled from prefabricated

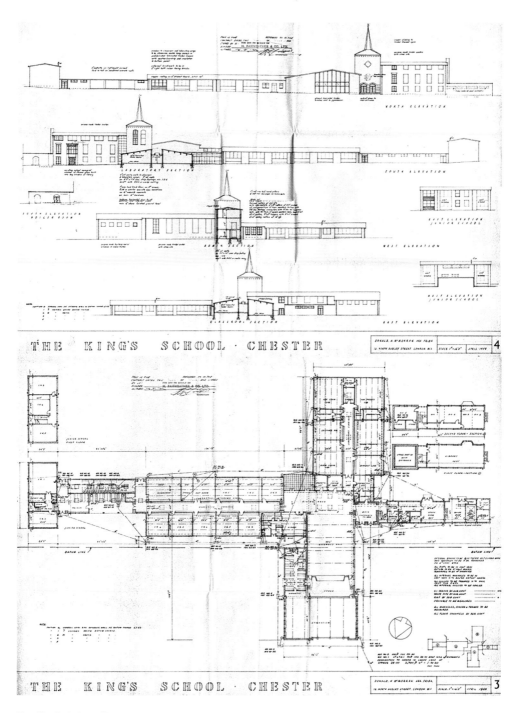

The King's School Chester plans, sections and elevations, 1956. The building was completed in 1960

The King's School Chester, 1957–60

components of reinforced concrete, cast on site in order to keep costs to a minimum. Another economical consideration by the architects was the inclusion of all openings for utilities, and mouldings for fixtures and fittings for the windows and roof, in the design of the pre-cast concrete components to avoid cutting the concrete after fabrication.

The modern design of Bow Road, replete with concrete and glass, is quite unlike anything Farquharson & McMorran attempted before or afterwards, but it is in no way antithetical to their views on design. Rather, it demonstrates their willingness to experiment with whatever materials and techniques delivered a viable solution. The concrete portal frame, filled with expansive sections of large windows covering three and sometimes four sides of the classroom block, provided a delicacy of structure and transparency that a compressive composition would struggle to achieve. The result is a series of contained, light and relaxed internal and external spaces that perform their functions interdependently, the outdoor spaces being for recreation and horticultural activities and the indoors for more formal learning. The school was awarded the London Architecture Bronze Medal in 1952.

Following Bow Road Open-Air School came an extension to the war-damaged Sir Walter St John's School in Battersea, London (1954), the Harlow schools in 1956, and new buildings at the Queen Elizabeth's School, Wakefield, and Cranbrook School, Kent, along with a new campus for The King's School, Chester (all 1957–66). The Battersea extension was commissioned by the LCC. It comprised nine classrooms and cloakrooms on three floors contained within a single block behind William Butterfield's Gothic edifice, and replaced a former classroom block designed by Ryan Tenison (1914) which had been severely damaged in an air raid in 1940. The Harlow schools were carried out in association with Harold Conolly (CBE, FRIBA), the County Architect for Essex from 1945 to 1966. At The King's School, Chester, the headmaster was the brother of McMorran's friend, Brian Harvey. The King's School had been located in the centre of town for 400 years, but was now being removed to a new 13-hectare (32-acre) out-of-town campus. McMorran's designs for it included everything from classrooms to sports pavilions, and from a library to a boathouse. He even made designs for the school gates, the first of which, in 1959, mirrored almost exactly the gate Farquharson had designed for McMorran's home in Dorking. McMorran even managed to secure the installation of a chandelier, costing £100, designed for Sir Edwin Lutyens's Viceroy's House at Delhi, which was hung in the entrance hall in time for the school's official opening by the Queen Mother on 22 June 1960.[5] Although McMorran found the school 'no easy client', work at the campus continued throughout the early 1960s, with subsequent designs for classroom extensions, staff residences and a swimming pool (1961–3).[6] The exterior form of the pool – with its miniature tower and low-lying wings of brick, glass and concrete – is conspicuously like that of the main building at Bow Road designed a decade earlier.

Notes

1   *Builder*, 21 October 1949, p513.
2   *Builder*, 28 March 1947, p294.
3   *Builder*, 21 October 1949, p513.
4   *Builder*, 24 October 1952, p581.
5   Letter from McMorran to the headmaster,

Mr Harvey, The King's School Archives, GB.3154. A2007/3/1.
6   Letter from Brian Harvey to William McMorran, 11 November 1997; courtesy of the McMorran family archive.

Flat Nos.
1 to 6

5 Passing the Flame

The 1950s represented a period of transition for Farquharson & McMorran that ultimately led to the practice's reincarnation as McMorran & Whitby. The grounds for this transition were laid some time before, in the type and extent of work coming into 14 North Audley Street, in the fortunes of colleagues and associates, and in the rekindling of old relationships. Above all, the steadily rising tide of work throughout the early 1950s put pressure on McMorran to choose either to expand the firm in order to meet the growing demands of larger jobs or to remain a small but specialised office focusing on select building types. The possibility of now adding substantial housing and school projects to the practice's already-established reputation for designing important public buildings appeared to be paying dividends, and the outlook from the start of the 1950s suggested that this was to be a seminal decade professionally.

However, while professional matters followed their course, the practice's transition was ultimately hastened by concerns far greater than the work. Nature was to intervene in ways that were both inevitable and horribly unpredictable. Firstly, Farquharson's advancing age caused him increasingly to retreat from the fray. He was in his eighties by the middle of the decade and so was little involved in seeking or executing commissions. Secondly, events in McMorran's private life forced his hand. Towards the end of 1956, his eldest daughter, Susan, was struck by polio. The news devastated the family. McMorran committed himself to seeking treatment for her, and she delayed her course at the Courtauld Institute to undergo costly treatment alone for six months in Switzerland – an experience that helped to cultivate her characteristically strong sense of independence and fortitude, and which consumed her father's concentration. Susan was a woman of remarkable poise and intellect, and although the polio paralysed her from the waist down, this did not deter her from pursuing a distinguished career in the Historic Buildings Division at the Greater London Council, or from writing on architecture. Her prolific research is most famously manifested in her pioneering and award-winning book about late 19th-century British sculpture, *The New Sculpture*.

While this very personal crisis was unfolding for McMorran, a professional crisis was unfolding for Whitby. His architectural experience to date had been his work at 14 North Audley Street and his employment with the firm Welch, Cachemaille-Day & Lander, but following his return from war service he joined the architectural firm Walters & Kerr Bate and soon became a partner. The practice duly changed its name to Walters, Whitby & Kerr Bate. Soon after accepting this position, Whitby received the opportunity to design his first ever building independently – a project that helped him to establish himself as a young architect of considerable promise, but which came at a considerable cost and caused consternation among his former partners. The project,

Opposite: Detail of flats, Lammas Green Estate, Lewisham, London, 1955–7

initiated in the late 1940s, was for a large secondary school on a bombed site in East London. However, strict cost limits on school building were imposed by the Labour Government, returned to power in early 1950, and the work that had been planned to start in 1951 was postponed. Five hectares (12 acres) of land had originally been designated to the project, but the demolition of the remaining houses and the resettlement of their residents proved complicated. Owing to the urgent need for a new school for girls, a site of less than 0.4 hectares (1 acre) was made available, with the provision for the boys' school to be added at a later date. In the meantime, the government revised existing regulations, permitting an increase in the numbers of girls on this site from 560 to 680. Consequently, the project was redesigned as a two-phase scheme to accommodate the total number of girls in the first phase of development and a similar number of boys in the second.

Excavation work started in June 1952, and on 26 November a ceremony was held that was billed as 'column casting' rather than foundation-stone laying. The modern parlance was fitting. With steel still rationed, the Ministry of Education could not provide enough of the material to allow the school to be built using standard reinforced concrete. The structural engineer, R. F. Galbraith, provided a unique and innovative solution that avoided further delays. With little more than 6 tonnes of steel available at the start of the project, the engineers chose to use pre-stressed concrete in the retaining walls, column bases and lower portions of the main columns. This allowed the project to start on schedule and made this the first time that such a technique was used for a school anywhere in the world. The successful pre-stressing technique used throughout the remaining elements consumed just 22 tonnes of steel compared with the 66 tonnes that normal reinforcement would have used, and made it 'a building of outstanding technical interest'.[1]

The other notable feature of the scheme was the high degree of standardisation in the plan and floor heights that helped to reduce significantly the extent of on-site work and allowed the use of pre-cast pre-stressed components, with window surrounds, staircases, posts, beams and floor slabs all slotting together and being bolted securely. This building work was carried out by the general contractors, Bernard Sunley & Sons.

Plashet County Secondary School for Girls, which was officially opened on 8 May 1954, consists of a seven-storey cruciform structure in a conspicuously modern idiom rising from a base of rough-cut Portland stone. The east and west wings were enlarged on the ground floor to accommodate an assembly hall and gymnasium respectively, while classrooms were arranged around the building's core (containing stairwells and two large lifts, each capable of holding half a class) so that each one receives cross-lighting and good ventilation. The younger children were to occupy the classrooms on the lower floors and the older children those on the upper floors, so that children would literally 'go up' the school in the years they spent there. A basement provided space for a boiler room and storage. Each floor was 3 metres (10 feet) high, with mezzanines occupying three of the four wings on the ground-floor level. To improve the building's acoustics, 50 mm (2 inches) of sand and 25mm (1 inch) of screed were laid above each floor plate to help deaden the sound from above.

Plashet School, East Ham, 1952–4

How Whitby received this prominent job so soon after returning from the war is not known. John Dyer, the Chief Education Officer in the East Ham Education Authority, may have been of assistance, while Dyer's brother-in-law – Alfred Harris, of Bunn, Groves and Harris – was the quantity surveyor on the job. This relationship between the architect and the client, although clearly amiable at the outset, deteriorated as the project progressed, and concluded somewhat acrimoniously. Both parties reached

Some of the McMorran & Whitby family outside the back of 14 North Audley Street, clockwise from left: Norman Walker, Yvonne Ward (née Saville), George Whitby, Violet Telfer and Betty Murray

the threshold over the late inclusion of a nuclear bunker, a disagreement that was not resolved until many years later when Whitby was vindicated. At the time, the client withheld all payments to the architect, a strategy that imposed considerable financial difficulties on Whitby.

The job also proved influential when the client, East Ham Borough Council, took the contractor, Bernard Sunley, to court over the failure of some of the fixings that held the cladding in place. The contractor had failed to grant Whitby access to inspect the fixings and refused to accept liability. The case eventually went to the House of Lords, where the client and Whitby were vindicated. It created a significant piece of case law for architects and builders alike concerning liability where inspection is deliberately denied.

Towards the end of the project, Whitby was in desperate need of work, not least to provide a degree of financial security for his rapidly growing family. He and Charmian had been blessed with the birth of their first child, Richard, in 1947 and five more children – Mary, Mark, Helen, Steven and Clive followed. It seems somehow apt following Whitby's technical successes at Plashet School that his second son, Mark, would go on to establish one of the leading engineering firms in Britain, Whitby & Bird, later Ramboll Whitbybird. Such achievements were a long way from the somewhat fraught circumstances in which Whitby senior found himself at this point in his career. He took work as a lecturer at Hammersmith College of Art for £4 per week, while pursuing architecture through competitions. He came third in the competition for a new secondary school at Hunstanton in 1950, won by Alison and Peter Smithson. The three shortlisted entries were, in the eyes of the assessor, the architect Denis Clarke Hall, 'the only ones that gave any real contribution to the problems of planning schools to the 1950 requirement'.[2] Whitby's proposal, which won him £150, was, like Plashet School, a cruciform design with classrooms based around a central stairwell.

With mounting pressure in his professional and private life, Whitby found a degree of security at 14 North Audley Street. In 1951, he set up his office in the top two floors, which, having been occupied during the war by American officers, were now vacant. Horace Farquharson's decision, back in 1907, to lease the entire property had proved decidedly perspicacious. By the early 1950s, Farquharson & McMorran were sub-letting to Josepou's, a shoe shop, on the ground floor and to Whitby on the top two floors, while they occupied the first and second floors. The arrangement suited everyone very nicely. Farquharson & McMorran, reunited at least physically with a former colleague, had reliable and familiar tenants, while Whitby had a permanent office and a reasonable rent. This proved all the more fortunate when the problems at Plashet School arose. Out of adversity emerged a solution with lasting consequences for the architectural family housed at 14 North Audley Street and for post-war British architecture in general. When he was unable to pay the rent Whitby was more than happy to receive jobs farmed out, or rather up, to him by McMorran, who was increasingly unable to cope with the demands imposed by the accumulating years of his partner, the increasing workload and his daughter's condition.

Also arriving with Whitby at 14 North Audley Street was his secretary, Betty Murray, who would move downstairs with Whitby in 1958 to replace Farquharson & McMorran's secretary, Miss Campbell. However, her role transcended that of a secretary, since it demanded the careful management of three men and the multitude of matters that made up the complex worlds perpetually whirling about them. Born in Poona, western India, Murray was the daughter of an army doctor and returned to England to undertake a degree in English Literature, first at Regent Street Polytechnic and then at University College London. After graduating in 1951, she applied for a temporary job through an agency, little knowing that her posting with Whitby would occupy the next 30 years of her life. During this time she became the linchpin at 14 North Audley Street and the only person to remain with the practice throughout.

By the early 1950s, therefore, all the principal characters who would come to play a role in the most prolific and profitable period experienced at 14 North Audley Street were installed, if not yet working collectively. Before Whitby became an established colleague to Farquharson & McMorran, he undertook work in Tripoli for the War Office, various private residences in south-west London, alterations to the Indonesian Ambassador's Residence and the Swiss Embassy, and a church in Northolt Grange that he designed in 1956 and the drawing for which appeared in the Royal Academy Summer Exhibition that year. Questions were initially raised about Whitby's joining McMorran. He was often said to be a little wild, but this exuberance complemented McMorran's discipline and Whitby's 'cheerful, enthusiastic and immensely likeable' character brought renewed energy to the office in the same way that McMorran had done when joining Farquharson two decades earlier.[3] In 1955, McMorran was described as being 'one of a small band of contemporary architects whose works have that special quality of strength, cohesion and sensitivity which, given good planning, marks the great building'.[4] Whitby brought even greater strength to the outfit.

The Foundation of the Practice

Farquharson & McMorran were recognised by the 1950s as an emerging force in the design of single buildings for public institutions and of larger schemes requiring more complex and extensive planning. The combination of these two very different scales of work brought about a number of major opportunities in the 1950s that would make McMorran, in particular, one of the most distinguished British architects of his generation. At the same time, he was making his way into the Establishment, a course that in hindsight might appear inevitable given his pedigree with Farquharson and Harris, themselves both well connected, and his strengthening bond with other key architects. Charles Holden wrote to McMorran in 1955 that he was 'impressed by your work and would like to see more of it ... I felt I must become better acquainted with you.'[5]

In April 1952, McMorran was appointed on to the Architectural Education Joint Committee (1952–4), which set out to assess the state of architectural education and recommend improvements. These were published in early 1955 as what the *Architects' Journal* termed 'The McMorran Report on education – known to fewer people as the Report of the Architectural Education Joint Committee on the Training and Qualification for Associate Membership of the Royal Institute of British Architects'.[6] McMorran cared passionately, almost fanatically, about the state of architectural education, advocating the need to 'get students back into offices, and as often as possible on to the [building] site, so that they can get to know the men who do the work and understand the materials used'.[7] It dismayed him terribly to witness how the RIBA increasingly 'indulged theory at the expense of practice'.[8] One of the report's approved recommendations was that students undertake a minimum of two years' practical experience (though McMorran's preference was three to four years), but 'resentments against the ideas expressed were responsible for the shelving of the report'.[9] Later, the architectural establishment realised the error it had made, and in 1962 performed a U-turn, from which it was said that McMorran 'must be deriving some wry pleasure'.[10]

Virtually all the opportunities that came into 14 North Audley Street during the 1950s came from public clients, and included housing, local government offices and educational institutions. Some were notably prestigious, among them an audacious high-rise proposal for the extension of the National Gallery in 1958 and a design for St Paul's Choir School in the City. Neither project was realised, though the latter caused

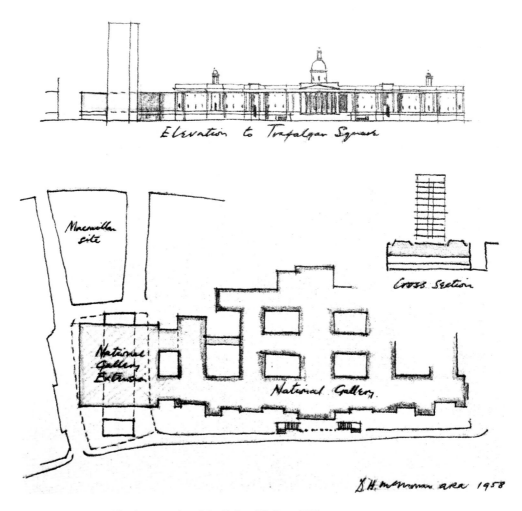

McMorran's proposal for the extension of the National Gallery, 1958

a degree of heartache. When initial designs for the Choir School submitted by Lord Mottistone – better known as John Seely of Seely & Paget, godson of Sir Winston Churchill – were rejected by the Royal Fine Arts Commission, the Dean and Chapter of St Paul's appointed McMorran to assist him in 1959. McMorran produced a three-storey circular plan for the site, which was completed in 1961, approved by the RFAC and forwarded to the Ministry of Housing and Local Government (MHLG) for approval. The MHLG, without rejecting McMorran's design, promptly initiated a competition for the project. McMorran was not invited to take part. The decision to initiate a competition was described as indicating 'a degree of high-handedness' by the Minister, Henry

McMorran's proposal for St Paul's Choir School, 1959–61
Plans for St Paul's Choir School. Ground floor (top left) clockwise, through first, second and third floor

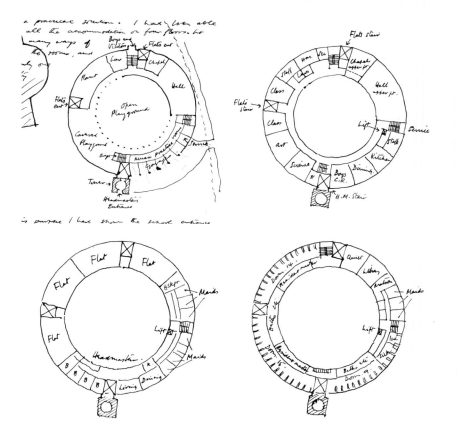

Brooke.[11] In 1961, when the description 'chequered' was used in reference to the history of the Dean and Chapter's search for an appropriate architect, this was suggested to be one of the 'architectural understatements of our time'.[12]

The genesis of most of the projects undertaken in the 1950s lay in some important, if sometimes diminutive, commissions the practice secured shortly after the war, as well as with the reputation the practice had made for themselves through their previous work, particularly at Hammersmith, which seems to have confirmed their position within the architectural community as a traditionalist firm. Three major works from this period stand out as seminal projects for which the practice would always be remembered: the Lammas Green Estate in south London, Devon County Hall, and halls of residence and departmental buildings at Nottingham University. However, it is too simplistic to single out influential designs in isolation while overlooking the wider context in which they were created. Each one overlapped the next, and consequently a common language emerged whose genesis lay in less prominent projects.

The Lammas Green Estate

The Lammas Green Estate is located on Sydenham Hill in the Borough of Lewisham, but was commissioned by the Corporation of the City of London who owned the land. Designed by McMorran in 1955 and opened on 1 November 1957, this estate draws on the very English tradition of the village green, yet it is not traditionalist. It appears as though a rural environment has been charmingly fashioned from a suburban context by placing a range of houses and flats around a central 'green', but while this might be the result it would not have been McMorran's intention. For this, one must again observe the planning. In spite of its apparent historical derivation, the sensitivity with which the plan has been executed caused it to escape the ire of the Modernists – and to surpass, as well as predate by half a century, the less-assured attempts by flag-wavers for conservatism in architecture and planning. As an exercise in planning it is robust enough to be scrutinised in isolation, but, far more importantly, its inclusive character augments the surrounding suburban environment. McMorran would have abhorred an inward-looking scheme that espoused the cosy insularity of middle-England, just as he was keenly aware of the failings of Modernist planning that turned its back on the real world in its pursuit of a utopian dream that rarely transcended a nightmare.

The 1.4-hectare (3½-acre) site on the south side of the busy Sydenham Hill Road was formerly occupied by three houses, two of which had been derelict since the war. Town planning regulations would have permitted as many as 70 dwellings on the site, but this was very wisely limited by the City to 57 'so as to establish the conditions under which a community with its own life and identity might be able to grow and flourish'.[13] While the three houses were to be demolished to make way for the new scheme, a number of mature and notably fine trees were to remain. This was one of the principal causes for developing the site around a central, communal space. The character of the site is marked by a steep slope descending from the main road southwards, which provided a sound basis for the picturesque arrangement of the development, comprising 27 houses and 30 flats, a community hall, garages and communal utilities such as laundry rooms and stores. McMorran positioned 2 three-storey buildings, containing flats, at the top of the site adjacent to the main road in order to provide a degree of protection for the rest. These two blocks are set at right angles to one another, the larger one forming one

Lammas Green Estate, 1955–7

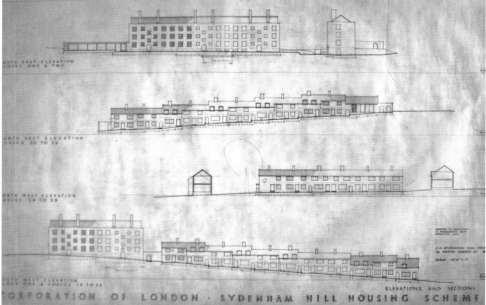

Drawings and elevations for Lammas Green Estate, 1955–7

House at Camilla Lacy, near
Westhumble, designed by McMorran,
c. 1947–52

side of the communal square. Between them passes the only access road into the site.
The remaining three sides of the square are occupied by two-storey houses finished
in whitewashed Essex brick under red-tiled pitched roofs, and all with rear gardens.
A community hall in the north-west corner is capable of seating up to 80 people.
Internally, the flats are arranged as one- or two-bedroom units and the houses are all
three-bedroom units with a living-room and 'dining-kitchen'.

The elements of this assorted scheme derive unmistakably from McMorran's stylistic
palette. The two blocks of flats in pale, bare brick evoke his Parkhill Road and Fellows
Road schemes, with their orderly fenestration and pitched roofs, concealed behind
parapets on the principal elevation, countered by the white-painted gable ends that
reveal themselves from the sides of the building. Here though, McMorran has revived
the large chimney stacks of Hammersmith – stouter in this incarnation, but nevertheless disciplined as they stand in regimented pairs imperiously overlooking the site.
Round arches, first seen at Currie House in Poplar, reappear at Lammas Green too, with
communal gateways and entrances to private residences forged in McMorran's favoured
form. The whitewashed walls of the private houses are not new either. Their genesis
stretches back to earlier works by McMorran near his home town of Dorking.

Farquharson & McMorran had designed several private houses in the village of
Westhumble, just outside Dorking, during the war and shortly after. Their whitewashed
walls, metal balcony railings and strong perpendicular lines, all viewed from an acute
angle, portrayed their structure as being decidedly modern. Although the reality was

far from avant-garde, the 'contemporary cottage' style of fresh, whitewashed brick was an effect that McMorran replicated in a scheme in central Dorking, at a site called Chequer's Yard.

Commissioned by Dorking Urban District Council, the Chequers Yard development consisted of 20 dwellings situated around a central green space, in which stood two mature trees that 'partly dictated the arrangements of the blocks'.[14] The scheme was designed for families and the elderly, and comprised two- and three-bedroom dwellings arranged in one- and two-storey blocks. The site had a fall of about 5 metres (16½ feet) from south to north, so the buildings were stepped down the hill either side of a public footpath. The exterior finish of common brick, painted with white cement paint, and metal casement windows produces an effect that – along with the topography, the design, the suburban setting, the planning, the composition and the detailed design – is a definite prototype for the Lammas Green Estate.

Perhaps the most important outcome of McMorran's work for the City at Sydenham Hill was not the exceptional quality of the architecture, which was awarded the status of Grade II listing in 1998, but the relationship that the job helped to build between architect and client. This contributed to the establishment of a partnership that would have a profound impact on the architecture of the City of London and would result in the two most important buildings to come out of 14 North Audley Street.

Chequers Yard, Dorking, 1950–2

Devon County Hall, Exeter

While McMorran was busy cultivating his position in the country's capital, his growing reputation for producing sincere, scholarly and humane buildings was also making him a sought-after figure further afield. McMorran's first major work outside London was at Exeter, where he was commissioned to design the new Devon County Hall.[15]

In 1952, the county council had purchased land in the parish of St Leonards, 2.4 kilometres (1½ miles) to the east of the city centre, with the intention of building new centralised offices on a site formerly owned by the Baring family (founders of Baring's Bank) and containing two significant houses, Bellair and Coaver. These two buildings, from the 18th and 19th centuries respectively, were the principal features of the landscaped site and would form the backdrop to the new offices. It was an ideal setting for McMorran's work. With very meagre available funds and a near moratorium on new offices for public institutions, the idea of a major new scheme for centralised offices for the county council seemed faintly fanciful. However, the matter became a political battle that was taken up by the council's clerk, the clearly impassioned H. G. Godsall.

In May 1954, Godsall met C. D. Spragg, Secretary of the RIBA, to discuss the matter and seek suggestions concerning which architects might be appropriate for the job. To provide some degree of guidance, Godsall wrote to Spragg, saying: 'The building obviously must have some relation to Exeter and probably the best represented style of architecture is Regency or Georgian.' He also made it clear what he did not want when he continued: 'I think therefore that any elevation in the modern style would probably be out of place, but we do want something which is really attractive and modern.'[16]

Spragg's reply suggested six architects: John Denman (1882–1975) & Sons, Julian Leathart (1891–1967), Donald McMorran, Stephen Rowland Pierce (1896–1966), Louis de Soissons (1890–1962) and Sir Hubert Worthington (1886–1963).[17] McMorran was the youngest on the list by a considerable margin and was far less a part of the architectural establishment, though this situation was then beginning to change quite rapidly. These options gave Godsall plenty of food for thought. Interestingly, Leathart had been the author of the glowing article about Hammersmith Police Station in the *Builder* in 1942, in which he adjudged McMorran's work to be 'one of the most successful compositions I have seen for a long time',[18] and Pierce had been the assessor for Marylebone Police Station for which Farquharson & McMorran were shortlisted in 1938.

Although McMorran was less experienced than the others on the list, he knew the importance of drawing heavily from his associations with his previous employers. In a letter to Godsall in June 1954, he tactically prodded: 'It may interest your Council to know that I received much of my training in the office of Mr. E. Vincent Harris RA, under whom I was engaged on the new Government Offices in Whitehall Gardens, the County Offices at Taunton and Kingston-on-Thames, and the buildings of Exeter University College.'[19] Harris had designed most of Exeter University to that date, and as a Devon man may have wielded some influence in architectural circles in the city.

From a shortlist of McMorran, de Soissons and Leathart, McMorran was awarded the job on 23 July 1954, the day after his interview. A week later, Leathart wrote to

Early concept sketch for Devon County Hall, Exeter, 1954–63

Concept sketch (1959) for Devon County Hall, Exeter (1954–63), showing the main entrance, Great Gateway, Council Chamber and tower

Godsall stating graciously: 'Mr McMorran is a friend of mine and I assure you that your committee could not have made a better choice. The County is assured of a scholarly and efficiently designed building.'[20]

So it was that McMorran won the 'plum job', as the *Architects' Journal* described it, of designing Devon County Hall. [21] But his victory was just the start. There followed many years of political wrangling, vacillation and penny-pinching, during which relationships would be sorely tested, but whose conclusion was a superb scheme possessing some exceptional architecture.

The Archive Block and Turkey Oak at Devon County Hall, Exeter, 1954–63

The two existing buildings on the site, Coaver and Bellair, together with 9 hectares (22 acres) of notable natural setting that comprised the former private grounds, offered McMorran a most picturesque canvas on which to begin drafting his designs, which he was already close to finalising by the middle of 1955. His earliest sketches suggest that he always intended to incorporate Coaver and Bellair into these plans, although the manner in which they appear in the final scheme reveals them heavily modified. Nevertheless, the sanctity of this charming scene was obviously a principal factor in McMorran's plans to safeguard the setting and achieve 'a "country house" atmosphere'.[22] He achieved this by confining much of the development to the north-east of the site, thereby not only preserving the expansive green areas to the south-west but also providing an attractive panorama over which the principal offices could look out – a location which he recognised to be 'an amenity and quite unique setting for a building of this type'.[23] McMorran knew he had been gifted a favourable site when, shortly after starting the project, he wrote to Godsall acknowledging the positive attributes by stating that 'nothing helps a building more than green lawns'. He was concerned not to undermine the setting. 'Nothing', he claimed, 'spoils a building so much as ranks of shiny cars.' It was imperative, therefore, to situate the car parking and other services in the north-east corner of the site.[24]

The general logic of this plan was visible in McMorran's first sketches, presented to the council committee in mid-1955. The council's Special Purposes Committee deemed the scheme too expensive and made suggestions to reduce costs, but by 1958 these

South elevation of the offices at Devon County Hall, Exeter, 1954–63

Bellair, connected to the clocktower, Devon County Hall, Exeter, 1954–63

parsimonious measures were challenged severely when, at the time construction works were due to start, the relevant departments that were to occupy the offices had grown to such an extent as to necessitate the design and construction of an annexe, the plans for which were drafted in 1959. This appendage, subsequently referred to discreetly as the 'Archive Block', was situated to the east of, and detached from, the main building. However, even this overflow office block did not escape the impecuniousness of the council committee: it was later reduced in size and lost one portion of its originally L-shaped plan. This pruning of space did, however, reprieve the large Turkey Oak, which still stands just south of the building.

The two principal materials proposed for the scheme were brick and stone, though the type of stone remained open. Portland stone was in short supply owing to the strong demand from London, making Devon granite the favoured option. McMorran proposed a brick of a golden-brown hue, similar to that which he had so often used in London that it was becoming his trademark. At Exeter, he used, characteristically, a handmade Ibstock golden-brown facing brick to shroud the reinforced-concrete superstructure within. The exceptional finish was achieved by using 'fat' and 'unpointed' mortar 'exactly as Lutyens and Vincent Harris would have done'.[25] The quality of finish, which McMorran always insisted upon and which Farquharson had stressed was such a vital part of their previous work, was achieved by the structural engineers on the project, W. V. Zinn & Associates. Over half a century later, the condition remains near perfect, which is remarkable when one considers that this is a concrete-frame building faced in brick with the consequent varying rates of expansion and contraction between these two materials.

At Exeter, McMorran's distinctive and familiar approach to using brick and stone was realised on a scale altogether larger than anything he had previously attempted. The whole structure is huge, with a complex plan whose principal element is the long central body that extends the full length of the site in an approximately north–south orientation. This contains ceremonial and members' rooms, with the council chamber set behind and a clock tower as its terminal feature. Two small wings protrude from the northern end of this 'spine', and include a corridor that connects it to Bellair, substantially remodelled and converted into a restroom for members. Approximately halfway along the central portion of the building on its east side, there extends a large perpendicular wing containing the council's various departmental offices and forming an open quadrangle with the southern half of the central building, in the manner of a lower-case 'h'. However, at the southern end of the central portion of the building another wing, also containing council offices, protrudes in a westerly direction. The result is a plan that gives ample opportunity for expressive elevations and a well-organised interplay between the different elements of the structure and the surrounding natural environment. The latter has been allowed to penetrate into, retreat from and 'touch' the scheme in the form of squares and gardens with varying degrees of intensity, formality and intimacy.

The composition and detailing of the exterior is varied throughout the different

The Council Chamber, Devon County Hall, Exeter, 1954–63

elements of the building, but is unified under one massive roofline that skirts the entire structure, a cohesive device interrupted only by the clock tower and the main entrance. Pinning this roof down on either side of the Great Gateway are two massive chimney stacks, typical of McMorran and evoking the work of Lutyens and Harris. As at Hackney, but unlike at Hammersmith, they have been turned perpendicular to the principal elevations, thereby presenting their slenderest profile to the façade, and offering ample gravity and depth when viewed tangentially. Again, McMorran has carefully considered the detailing of the chimneys, but here he has also added granite dressings as a form of entablature, a device he repeats on the top of the clock tower. Granite was used throughout the exterior for the slim plinth on the lower ground floor, string courses, lintels and arches. Shortly after the building had been completed, one article, positing rare approval and showing equally rare perspicacity, claimed it to be '… an able and confident essay in a domestic vernacular owing much to the late Georgian period'.[26]

The varied character of the different elevations reflects their purpose and is influenced by their function and topography. The more formal areas of the building are to the north, and face both west and east, the western elevation being the most formal since it faces the landscaped gardens, whereas the eastern elevation contains the main entrance. Penetrating the building from east to west and linking these two formal areas is the Great Gateway, a composition of three segmental-arched openings for vehicular

Railing detail at the main entrance of Devon County Hall, Exeter, 1954–63

The Great Gateway, Devon County Hall, Exeter, 1954–63

access flanked by two smaller, square-arched openings for pedestrians. Internally, these openings are united by very fine, low, vaulted ceilings supported on stocky square columns faced in granite. Such vaulting would reappear at the rear of the extension to the Central Criminal Court on London's Old Bailey a decade later.

Around the more functional parts of the building to the south, McMorran has incorporated small semi-circular ventilation grilles that protrude from the shallow-pitched expanses of slate. Their alignment is strictly determined by the fenestration beneath, which maintains the same orderly appearance as occurs on the southern end of the west elevation – only here the elevations are far larger and so the rhythm is broader, arranged in triplets where a large bay (of either eight or ten windows) is flanked on either side by two smaller bays containing three columns of windows. Within the courtyard and on the eastern elevation of the perpendicular arm of the building, McMorran has chosen to accentuate this rhythm by furnishing the top-floor windows of the middle bays with segmental-arched openings.

The sheer scale of the main building and its diverse gardens, car-parking areas, pedestrian access, open land, screen walls, enclosed quadrangles and open courtyards demanded disciplined and well-executed landscaping. The attention to detail in the landscaping reflects McMorran's view that this part of the scheme should be 'seen as part of the design of the building', and it was carried out by McMorran and his office to the high standard that 'one would expect from architects of their pedigree'.[27] Internally the quality of materials, finishes and detailing is evident throughout and exemplified in the grand staircase, which possesses Ionic columns in Ashburton marble supporting a finely curved plaster vault. The finishes were said at the time to 'match up to the excellence of their Georgian antecedents' while the craftsmanship was said to be 'everywhere of a very high quality'.[28] McMorran designed the interior fittings and furnishings of the council chamber, which was lined in walnut.

The building was planned to open in August 1961, but delays caused it to open in stages, from October 1961 to 1963. After working on it for nearly a decade, McMorran – and no doubt Godsall, too – were reaching the limits of their patience. The relationship between these two men 'was of key importance to the project', but having remained formal though with obvious signs of friendship, towards the end of the project there was a noticeable shift in attitude.[29] By this time, both were delegating responsibilities to their other staff: Godsall to officers of separate council departments and McMorran to Whitby, who was, by then, the architect responsible for supervising the building works.

A similar combination of materials, applied by the same engineers in a design by McMorran & Whitby, was used a few years later for the new Folkestone Council Offices and Chamber. Rather uncharacteristically, this scheme included a nine-storey, 30-metre (100-foot) high tower block surrounded by garden courtyards, and council chamber and mayor's parlour suite. A reinforced-concrete frame faced in Dorking bricks with 'extensive use being made of Portland-stone facings'[30] was among the few elements to provide a clue that this scheme came from 14 North Audley Street.

As the works at Exeter came to a close, McMorran was engaged in major works

Left: The massive piers supporting the Great Gateway

Above: (left to right) Alexander McMorran, Mr Cox (site agent), George Whitby, Mr Williamson (Clerk of Works) at Exeter presiding over the base of the columns due to support the Great Gateway

Corridor of the Meeting Rooms above the Great Gateway

The Ionic columns in Ashburton marble inside Devon County Hall, Exeter

McMorran's preliminary sketch proposals for Folkstone Civic Centre (1961), showing a marked resemblance to his second scheme for York Civic Centre

McMorran's later sketch proposal for Folkstone Civic Centre, 1962

elsewhere and so could not devote the necessary time to the manifold details that needed attention in the last stages of the project. These included minutiae such as the design of the display cabinets for the Weights and Measures Department; and the requirements of the Poultry Instructresses, who needed somewhere to 'pluck fowls, burn refuse, and wash their pots and pans'.[31] Some of the furnishings and furniture were decidedly opulent, but the request for the council's crest to be embossed on the council-chamber chairs produced an emphatic 'no' from McMorran.

Nevertheless, the project was completed in 1964 at a cost of £1.5 million. Shortly afterwards, it was 'numbered amongst the very best' of those buildings whose style was 'rooted in an established aesthetic, or is exploratory and futuristic', either one of which is 'valid so long as they adequately fulfil their purpose'.[32] This legitimacy seems more than justified, since the building not only still serves its purpose admirably but appears to mature with age while admiration for it grows. As Jeremy and Caroline Gould surmise, those responsible for commissioning Devon County Hall 'were wise in the choice of their architect although it may have taken forty years for this to be understood'.[33] In 1954, Godsall had written a memo to his colleagues on the council stating that the building should be in a 'dignified sort of style, but incorporating perhaps some suitable modern touches in design'.[34] By 1964, McMorran had given them 'exactly the building they demanded and much more'.[35] It comes as little surprise, then, that in the third millennium many are looking back at this building and concluding that 'Devon County Hall confirms McMorran as an underrated master of an undervalued genre',[36] one that 'represents the end of a tradition that was fluent in visual architectural history, [and which] understood the need to continue to innovate but also understood that it was not necessary to re-invent the architectural wheel'.[37]

Nottingham University

While the plans for Devon County Hall were on the drawing board, designs for a new hall of residence at Nottingham University were already well under way. Indeed, McMorran's increasing commitments at Nottingham (and elsewhere) were one of the causes for the deteriorating relationships at Exeter by the early 1960s. However, the parallel projects also offered a degree of mutual benefit, where lessons learned in one could usefully inform the other. This was particularly true on the point of materials, and it was over the choice of materials for Devon County Hall that Godsall and McMorran took a trip to Nottingham in the summer of 1959 to visit the practice's recently completed Cripps Hall. This used a similar combination of materials to that which was proposed for Devon County Hall: golden-brown bricks, Westmorland slate for the roofs, and stone for the facings, lintels, sills and string courses. After this trip, Godsall returned to Exeter to report to the council committee, confidently proclaiming their selection of 'brick, stone and slate' to be 'without doubt an excellent one'. Cripps Hall was, undeniably, an excellent 'sales pitch' for McMorran.

There are more similarities between these two contemporaneous projects than just the materials. In their planning, Cripps Hall and Devon County Hall are founded on the disciplined arrangement of comparatively low-rise buildings around a courtyard or formal open space composed within a quasi-rural setting. In their design, both employ brick and stone to create distinguished and orderly elevations set beneath shallow-pitched roofs of slate, on which stand, for dramatic effect, hefty chimney stacks. Both schemes also boast conspicuous clock towers.

The genesis of McMorran's professional association with Nottingham University lies in the early 1950s, but may go back much further. In 1925, McMorran was working as a young student in the offices of Morley Horder, and would have seen or even contributed to Horder's designs for the university. Sir Jesse Boot paid for the University College, Nottingham, to move in the 1920s to its new suburban site. Horder designed Florence

Boot Hall for women in 1926–8, along with the administrative Trent Building and Hugh Stewart Hall for men (an extension of the old Lenton Hall made in 1930–2), which has some affinity with McMorran's work.

The numerous buildings constructed after the war on Nottingham University's new campus were part of an ambitious plan devised in 1949 by Sir Percy Thomas, former RIBA President and consultant architect to the university. This document was super-seded by a second plan in 1955 by Geoffrey Jellicoe, which drew on Thomas's basic concept. However, rather than rely on the axial plan of the latter it emphasised the positioning of the university's key buildings on a peninsula-like formation encircled by a green belt, outside which he refined Thomas's arrangement of halls of residence in an arc – with halls for men to the north and east, and for women to the west. It was the design of the buildings on this 'peninsula' that concentrated attention from Thomas, Jellicoe and McMorran in turn, since this constituted the heart of the campus and its layout was deemed integral to the subsequent success, or failure, of the entire project. Although the form of Jellicoe's plan was more progressive than Thomas's Beaux Arts-inspired ideas, the design of individual buildings within the peninsula and the halls of residence remained markedly conservative until the 1960s – a consequence, apparently, of the predilection of Thomas and the University's Vice-Chancellor, Bertrand Hallward.

Into this environment stepped a number of ostensibly traditionalist practitioners who would furnish the campus with an eclectic mix of buildings over the next decade. These were criticised by the contemporary architectural press for being too conven-tional, but the university deemed that modern architecture in the 1950s could not produce the 'collegiate atmosphere' it sought. The *Architects' Journal* belittled the results as 'classical ornaments' with 'rather the air of white sugar decorations on a cake'.[38] This remark was aimed at the assortment of designs for halls of residences commissioned in 1960; among them was McMorran's design for Lenton Hall. The *Builder* even dismissed McMorran's earlier, more refined, Cripps Hall somewhat churl-ishly by stating: 'Quite what Donald McMorran is trying to remember … is hard to say, but he has presented a very pretty drawing of his thought.'[39] Nevertheless, despite this apparently motley collection of designs, time has permitted the mellowing of emotions and a former head of the University School of Architecture has suggested that 'of all the architects brought in to realise Bertrand Hallward and Sir Percy Thomas' vision of the campus, the most interesting and undoubtedly the best were the firm of McMorran & Whitby'.[40]

The decision to build Cripps Hall was announced in late 1956 and construction started a year later. It was named after the benefactor Mr Cyril Cripps, who together with his son, Humphrey (benefactor of St John's College and Queens' College, Cambridge, for modern buildings by Powell & Moya in the 1960s and 1970s), ran a very successful automotive parts factory near Northampton and who donated £400,000 of the £500,000 needed to build the hall of residence. It was their firm belief that it was 'essential for students to reside within the precincts of the university so that they may have the fullest opportunity of benefiting from the atmosphere which a place of culture

McMorran with Cyril and Humphrey Cripps, viewing a model of Cripps Hall

provides'.[41] Nottingham was at that time sorely lacking in halls of residence. The Cripps family had contributed funds to other departments of the university, but its members felt that the provision of first-class halls was a priority and they were the first private donors after the war to offer funding for the type of buildings they felt students needed. At the stone-laying ceremony, Hallward acknowledged the substantial gift made by the Cripps family, a contribution that is evidenced clearly in the final design, which is more complete, more embellished and more accomplished than McMorran's subsequent works at Nottingham. Hallward went on to affirm somewhat prophetically that: 'It is my earnest desire and hope that from this stone will rise buildings that throughout the years to come will not only provide amenities and comforts for many thousands of students, but will be for the general benefit of our country.' These sentiments were echoed upon the building's inauguration on 15 October 1959, when McMorran warmly recognised the significant difference this generous gift had made to the overall quality of the scheme by stating in the local press that 'the donors spared nothing in their aim to make the buildings no less beautiful and successful than the colleges at Oxford and Cambridge'.

Situated between Hugh Stewart and Wortley Halls, both adaptations of 19th-century villas that retained many specimen trees, the location for Cripps Hall was claimed by

Hallward to be 'one of the finest sites in University Park'. Designed to accommodate approximately 200 students, Cripps Hall comprises two quadrangles, around which its seven main blocks are arranged, with ancillary buildings behind. The topography of the site offers a gentle slope away from the main entrance so that the two quadrangles are set at different levels and the surrounding buildings are also of different heights ranging from one to three storeys. McMorran used Clipsham stone and opted once again for his familiar, narrow golden-brown bricks, although, unlike at Exeter, the 50 mm (2 inch) Leicester bricks for Cripps are loadbearing and do not rely on an internal reinforced-concrete frame. The decision to erect the building from loadbearing brick is said to have reduced both the cost and the construction time, which was just 21 months.

The composition comprises a refectory, library, common rooms, staff block, warden's house and student accommodation, all organised in a manner evidencing great skill and sensitivity in the planning and in the use of traditional materials, which are remarkably well suited to their purpose and place. Entry to the site is provided from the north-west through a formal gateway named, somewhat pompously, the 'Gate of Honour'. This leads through to the first, and most formal, of the two grassed quadrangles, around which are situated the refectory, or Great Hall, and one student accommodation block. The quadrangle was open on the south-east side to provide views of the Trent Valley from the quadrangle and from the main entrance, which framed the view as though a work of art. On either side of the Gate of Honour are, on the ground floor, senior common rooms, seminar rooms, guest accommodation and offices and, on the first

Refectory, Cripps Hall, Nottingham University, 1957–9

The Gate of Honour, Cripps Hall, 1957–9

floor, porter's lodgings and a flat for married dons. McMorran sought to unify both wings either side of this entrance by continuing the roofline across the entire width of the quadrangle, a scheme perhaps inspired by a similar design by Lutyens for the stable block at Great Maytham Hall in Kent. Throughout the scheme, McMorran has used shallow roofs of Westmorland slate almost concealed by stone parapets containing hidden drainage systems. Solid chimney stacks rise boldly to a considerable height from these slender rooflines in a manner that confirms McMorran's growing confidence in his visual vocabulary. He placed four Ionic columns in the Gate of Honour. He was particularly fond of the Ionic order, as it was the only directional order and thus befitted a gateway through which traffic flowed, the standard for this being set by the interior of the Propylaea of the Acropolis. McMorran provides his own simplified take on this classical form by removing the base. The stone from which these beautifully fashioned columns and capitals were carved possesses an almost magical quality – changing tone with the weather. Such beauty was lost on a sorry band of architectural radicals, named 'Anti-Ugly Action', who, in protest at their classical derivation, painted these four columns bright white in deference to Corbusier's pilotis. However, McMorran, more than most, understood the frustrations of the younger generation of architects: 'Some students are campaigning noisily against bad buildings (and, I say, good luck to them). What they are really fighting is lazy, slovenly thinking in architecture. I am rather afraid these students think this is just a question of style; but it is not as easy as that.'[42]

To the north of this entrance, and outside the quadrangular plan, a two-storey warden's lodge of charming simplicity sits beneath a pyramid roof crowned by a characteristic chimney stack. This delightful lodge is physically attached to the outer corner of the first quadrangle by a short corridor containing three segmental-arched windows in a screen wall, doubtless familiar to those working at Devon County Hall.

Inside the first quadrangle, on the north side stands the Great Hall and on the east and south is student accommodation. The Great Hall, with its distinctive tower bearing a clock and carillon, is the most formal of the buildings that make up the scheme. The double-height hall is lit by six tall, segmental-arched windows set in recessed brickwork. Ornament has been kept to a minimum, visual interest being aroused instead by a masterful display of massing, proportion and scale. The building is effectively divided into two parts – on the ground floor, the galleried refectory and the entrance, on either side of which are an ante-room and a junior common room; and on the first floor, the library – but the impact of this has been deliberately subdued by the unifying gesture of the single roof, stone entablature and beautifully crafted expanses of brickwork that wrap around, without interruption, the building's exterior. The brick tower is carefully

The Warden's Lodge (left) and Gate of Honour (right) showing the tower of the Great Hall in the background, 1957–9

Interior of the Great Hall, 1957–9

composed to appear supported by diminishing masses from the ground to its apex. However, at ground and first-floor levels there is no mass at all, but instead dark voids created by the archways that serve as entrances into the building. The segmental-arched openings are repeated throughout this composition to further provide cohesion to the overall arrangement, with two pairs of arches on the ground and first floors and a single arch in the uppermost section of the tower to reveal the bell. At the top of the tower, inscribed in brick, is the name of the contractor's agent, Mr S. D. Thompson, 'a tribute paid by the architects', above which stands a golden ball and weathervane crowning the structure. Inside, all furniture and fittings are designed by McMorran, including the tables, chairs and guarea-panelled ceiling lined in gold leaf. Behind the Great Hall are the kitchens and warden's house.

The Great Hall provides the starting point for one of the principal axes on which the scheme is based. This axis forms the link between the two quadrangles, which are joined at their corners. A series of steps leads down from the south side of the first quadrangle to the north side of the second, around which are situated four buildings providing student accommodation. Each accommodation block contains approximately 34 rooms over three floors with up to twelve 13 square metre (140 square foot) rooms to a floor, and each floor being divided in two equal parts with one bathroom and pantry serving each part. Some rooms with en-suite facilities were provided for dons. The elevations of these blocks are similar, all being symmetrically composed with two entrances each leading to a staircase that serves one half of the building. This arrangement appears externally throughout the fenestration, which is organised in rows of eight windows and, on the ground floor, six windows and two doors. Very little detailing appears on the elevations of these blocks, the sash windows being set in white hardwood frames; doors are framed in stone architraves, each with slightly different detailing; and a stone parapet encircles the entire block and conceals the guttering. In order to create a sense of enclosure, within each quadrangle, single-storey storage facilities were used to join the accommodation blocks.

View from the bottom of the second quadrangle looking up towards the Gate of Honour, Cripps Hall, 1957–9

Upon completion, this project was published under the broad banner of
Farquharson, McMorran & Whitby, but this scheme is quintessential McMorran.
Chronologically, as with Devon County Hall, it bridges the period between Farquharson
& McMorran and McMorran & Whitby, and reflects the firm's metamorphosis.
Farquharson remained a consultant until his death in 1966. McMorran's death the year
before prompted letters of appreciation from his Nottingham clients. The building
officer, Mr D. O'Dell, wrote to McMorran's widow, Margaret, stating that 'he not only
gained our respect for his qualities as an architect, but also our regard for the kind and
generous way in which he endeavoured to help us … this feeling of respect and affection
towards him extended far beyond this particular Department.'[43] The previous day, the
Acting Vice-Chancellor, Prof. Haycocks, had written a similarly appreciative letter
claiming McMorran's 'services to us were quite outstanding'.[44] It was unfortunate that
neither was around in 1968, when an extension to Cripps was planned and carried out
by Cartwright, Woollatt and Partners, who positioned three additional buildings to the
south-east of the upper quadrangle, thus obstructing the spectacular views of the Trent
valley that McMorran had deliberately intended to provide from the main entrance and
quadrangle, and shattering the axial planning that had offered such delicate formality
to the spatial quality of the scheme. Such problems were anticipated by the *Architects'
Journal* in 1960, which, despite being consistently critical of the type of architectural
style proposed at Nottingham, forewarned that 'the present solution might well destroy
the magnificent landscape of the University Park, if the student population rises much
above the [projected] 1968 figure of 4,000'.[45]

The craftsmanship on the building is exquisite, with the brickwork, stone carving
and interior woodwork all being carried out with evident pride and devotion. These
traits are lacking in the sorry execution of alterations demanded by contemporary
health-and-safety standards, which have required a new doorway to be punched
through the façade of the refectory, the stonework and pointing around which are of
a pitifully poor quality and are already failing after just one decade. It is unfortunate
to see that the stone coping has degraded too, causing the knife-edge sharpness of the
original to be blunted by a blanket of lead intended to protect it.

Following Cripps Hall, McMorran & Whitby embarked on the design of the university's Social Science Building (now the Law and Social Sciences Building; education
has moved to the new Jubilee campus). The designs for this new departmental building
were exhibited at the Royal Academy in 1958, and construction started the following
July, taking just 18 months to complete. Unlike Cripps and, later, Lenton halls, the
Social Science Building was located in the heart of the university, which was planned
as a piazza according to Jellicoe's 1955 revision of Thomas's plan, which McMorran had
attempted to update in 1958. Therefore, 'the siting and form of this building [had] been
carefully studied so as to contribute to the total effect' of this plan, and it comprises
the north-western boundary of the large piazza that was to form its core.[46] Defining the
southern boundary of this proposed piazza was Horder's Trent Building (1922–8) and
T. C. Howitt's Portland Building (1949–56). Unfortunately, the plan was never realised

The former Social Science Building, Nottingham University, 1958–60

and so McMorran & Whitby's Social Science Building remains somewhat detached in context. Its plan is an approximate 'U' shape, with a central portion facing the proposed piazza and two lengthy wings behind. At the northern end of the front elevation was a single-storey building attached to the façade, containing a lecture theatre. The topography was such that the main building was positioned on a gentle gradient behind the main façade, its two wings extending out from behind the main building somewhat forlornly down the hill in an unwanted embrace, until recently enclosed following the construction of a well-executed extension by Dykes Naylor. Despite this, the main body of the building looks out upon nothing – instead of the grand, anticipated formal piazza.

The size of the structure reflects its function of containing various university departments on different floors. McMorran & Whitby sought to differentiate between the departments by providing a degree of visual variety in the different elevations and between the floors. The principal elevation, for example, is three storeys, with a cloister serving the ground floor (which at this point is really a lower-ground floor); segmental-arched windows on the first floor and smaller rectangular windows on the

The former Social Science Building, Nottingham University, 1958–61

Sketch of the former Social Science Building (1958), Nottingham University, showing the two wings stretching out behind the principal façade

second floor; while the fenestration on each of the wings is characterised by a ground floor of segmental-arched windows, separated by stone dressings, with two upper floors of rectangular windows. However, the often strict alignment and proportions of the windows that McMorran employed in some of his other work are dissipated here, with tall windows, which serve internal stairwells, breaking the alignment of the rows of fenestration, and, somewhat inexplicably, varied heights of certain windows in each

Edmunds when the council requested, not unreasonably, larger windows to provide more natural light into the offices.

Later that year, McMorran & Whitby revised the design for the office block to accommodate the larger windows, and in so doing moved the main entrance to the western elevation, beneath the clock tower. To help define the elements of the office block within this new plan, they set back the portion of the building to the north of the entrance. This served to provide a break in the long roofline and offered a change in rhythm to the fenestration, while also giving the main entrance a more stately posture surrounded by an expanse of plain brick extending from the floor to the eaves. These plans suffered a setback in early 1960 when the Ministry of Housing and Local Government capped all loans for new office buildings until they had been reviewed by the Local Government Commission. To circumvent this new provision, West Suffolk County Council was permitted to proceed with their plans only if they were undertaken in stages. The result, in August 1960, was a scaled-down version of the original offices, a separate block for the police station (located to the south of the office block), and the library (still to the west of the road), which was the first of the three major blocks for which detailed plans were prepared.

Construction of both the police headquarters and the library proceeded in 1962, the former being completed in August 1964 and officially opened on 9 October, and the latter completed in May 1965. Both buildings (and, eventually, the offices too) were built of loadbearing brick faced with Leicestershire bricks and Portland stone dressings, with

The Library, Bury St Edmunds, 1965

Welsh slate on the roof. The police headquarters was a simple scheme of four buildings arranged in a square: the police station at the front, facing the main road, with the three minor buildings (garages, boiler house and workshops) concealed behind. Comprising two storeys, the symmetrical building was designed and constructed to accommodate an extra floor if necessary. The building's long façade has been arranged in three portions: the centre, containing the main entrance, and two identical wings – all sitting under a long slate roof, from which protrude, somewhat uncomfortably, two conspicuous round-arched louvre vents. The central portion, marked by six tall segmental-arched openings, contains the entrance lobby and reception on the ground floor and private offices of senior staff on the first floor. The entablature of Portland stone (which is balanced against a base of stone equal in depth running the length of the building) has been breached by the curved arc of each segmental-arched window and also underneath each vent, below which is a section of unbroken brickwork (save for a single short segmental-arched window and a characteristic blue police-station lamp on either side) separating the central portion from the two wings.

The wing to the north of the entrance contains kitchens, a dining room, a canteen and clothes stores, and the wing to the south has offices for training and various police departments. On the upper floors are private offices and a conference room. The ground-floor windows are all short, and set within recessed brick arches that mirror the tall openings in the central portion of the building, while the corresponding first-floor windows are rectangular and sit beneath the entablature. All windows sit on sills of Portland stone. The overall effect presented by the arrangement of the façade, although clean, is somewhat fragmented and lacks the clarity of better works such as Exeter or Cripps Hall.

Conversely, the library, across the road, is simpler, less adventurous and finer for it. The two-storey symmetrical façade stands high above the street, and so is accessed by a raised platform that leads around the corner to the car-parking area on the south side of the building. McMorran & Whitby employed elements here similar to those on the police station (Portland stone entablature, base and sills; recessed brickwork; segmental-arched openings), but the results are more gratifying. Five rectangular windows serve the first floor, with corresponding windows and a central doorway serving the ground floor. Two small wings of just one storey, containing recessed arched niches, balance the façade and hint at the wider ground-floor plan behind. A glazed cupola stands in the centre of the slate roof to provide light into the building's central stairwell. The northern and southern elevations use brickwork to provide a sense of rhythm, the wide segmental-arched windows sitting in recessed sections of brick, between narrower protruding sections containing round-arched niches of the same height. The building is only half the length it was designed to be, since the council chamber, meant for the western end of the library, was never built.

By the time the police station was nearing completion, a new and larger scheme for the office block was being finalised. This plan, published in June 1964, necessitated the demolition of St Margaret's to accommodate a larger northern portion of the office block, whose plan was now T-shaped, with the addition of an arm at the southern

Former West Suffolk County Council Library (left) and Council Offices (right)

West Suffolk Council Offices and main entrance, completed in 1968

end which had been reversed to face east, away from the road. The plans comprised a five-storey structure that, owing to the gradient falling away to the east, meant that the western elevation, containing the main entrance, actually appeared to be of four storeys, the lower-ground floor elsewhere being treated in a similar manner to the ground floor of the police station and the sides of the library – having recessed brick arches containing segmental-arched windows giving the impression of a colonnade. The design was markedly similar to simultaneous proposals for a civic centre at Tonbridge by McMorran, for which he was shortlisted and awarded £400 but did not win. The enlarged fenestration at Tonbridge, similar in style to that on the revised proposals for the offices at Bury St Edmunds, compromised almost the building's entire surface, which, if finished in brick or stone, would have appeared almost skeletal. A familiar tower, like that at Bury St Edmunds, crowned the proposal, but in the form of a carillon rather than a clock.

Bury St Edmunds's clock tower remained a part of the plan until 1966, when controls on government funding hindered progress once again and the project was delayed until the second half of the year. By this time, the design had been significantly altered and compromised. The preponderance of lintels with slightly jarring angled sides – first used at The King's School, Chester (1958–60), but reappearing at Lenton Hall (1962) – detracted from the rectilinear composition of the fenestration, which possesses a curious change of rhythm between the top floor and the lower floors. For every four windows on the lower floors, the top floor has five, a rhythm that is alluded to by the segmental-arches of every fifth window on the top floor encroaching into the entablature.

Economy perhaps undermined this scheme, delivering the final blow when plans submitted to the council in September 1966 showed that only the southern half of the offices were to be constructed and, the following month, the removal of the clock tower. Construction finally began in August 1966 and the building, providing 4,500 square metres (48,200 square feet) of office space, was opened on 16 October 1968. The second phase, which was intended to be constructed 'as soon as practicable', was never built, leaving the office block compromised, bland and boxy. [50] With the death of McMorran in 1965, it was up to Whitby and the Hungarian architect, senior assistant and Olympic basketball player, Tibor Cselko, to complete the designs of the office block. When the assessor for the Tonbridge Civic Centre, Reginald Uren, was unable to select a winner from six proposals, he said of McMorran's entry that 'there is no reason whatever why the architectural solution should not be found in the traditional manner but in this case the skill and scholarship of the author has not been applied sufficiently to the process of study and simplification which must be inherent in successful essays of this nature.' The same could be said, four years later, of the offices at Bury St Edmunds.

Notes

1   *Building*, 16 January 1953, p40

2   *Builder*, 12 May 1950, p642.

3   *Building*, 2 March 1973, p60.

4   *Builder*, 29 April 1955, p698.

5   Letter from Charles Holden to McMorran, 15 October 1955; courtesy of the McMorran family archive.

6   *Architects' Journal*, 10 February 1955, p195.

7   Donald McMorran, 'Everyday Things from the Architect's View Point', lecture, *op. cit.*

8   *Builder*, 13 August 1965, p331

9   ibid.

10 *Builder*, 9 November 1962, p913.

11 *Builder*, 6 April 1962, p699.

12 ibid.

13 *Builder*, 22 November 1957, p906.

14 *Builder*, 15 January 1954, p101.

15 For much of the information about Exeter County Hall, I am indebted to Jeremy and Caroline Gould and their excellent report: 'Listed Building Management Guidelines for Devon County Hall', unpublished, April 1999.

16 Letter from H. G. Godsall to Spragg, dated 17 May 1954, in Gould, *op. cit.*, p4.

17 Prior to the interviews, Worthington withdrew owing to his commitments elsewhere; Sir William Holford (1907–75) and William Curtis Green (1875–1960) were added to the list.

18 Julian Leathart, *Builder*, 12 December 1942, p272.

19 Letter from McMorran to Godsall, dated 10 June 1954, in Gould, *op. cit.*, p6.

20 Letter from Julian Leathart to Godsall, dated 29 July 1954, in Gould, ibid., p6.

21 Astragal, *Architects' Journal*, 6 May 1954, p539.

22 Letter from McMorran to Godsall on 14 September 1954, in *op. cit.*, p9.

23 McMorran quoted in the *Express and Echo*, 21 March 1955, in ibid., p. 9.

24 Letter from McMorran to Godsall, dated 14 September 1954, in ibid., p.9

25 ibid., p23.

26 H. A. N. Brockman, 'Devon's New County Hall – An Essay in the Georgian', *Financial Times*, 14 July 1964.

27 Gould, *op. cit.*, p15.

28 Brockman, *op. cit.*

29 Gould, *op. cit.*, p15.

30 *Building*, 29 June 1966, p79.

31 Letter, dated 21 December 1961, from Education Officer, W. E. Philip, to a Mr Timms in Gould, *op. cit.*, p16.

32 Brockman, *op. cit.*

33 Gould, *op. cit.*, pp19–20.

34 Memo from Godsall to Haynes, Shelley and Day, in ibid., p4.

35 ibid., pp19–20.

36 Elain Harwood, *England: A Guide to Post-War Listed Buildings*, Second Edition, London, B.T. Batsford, 2003, p336.

37 Gould, *op. cit.*, pp19–20.

38 *Architects' Journal*, 23 June 1960, p963.

39 *Builder*, 8 May 1959, p844.

40 A. Peter Fawcett and Neil Jackson, *Campus Critique – The Architecture of the University of Nottingham*, Nottingham, Sherwood Press, 1998, p74.

41 *The Times*, 16 October 1959.

42 Donald McMorran, 'Everyday Things from the Architect's View Point', lecture, *op. cit.*

43 Letter from D. O'Dell to Margaret McMorran, 11 August 1965; courtesy of the McMorran family archive.

44 Letter from Prof. Norman Haycocks to Margaret McMorran, 10 August 1965; courtesy of the McMorran family archive.

45 *Architects' Journal*, 23 June 1960, p963.

46 *Builder*, 12 January 1962, p65.

47 Letter from E. Vincent Harris to McMorran, 20 August 1942; courtesy of the McMorran family archive.

48 Handwritten note by McMorran on a letter from Dr Simpson, Headmaster of Harrow County School, to McMorran, 7 March 1960; courtesy of the McMorran family archive

49 CA/PL Radford Boulevard, 165/9/65, John Player Offices, Nottinghamshire Archives, courtesy of Elain Harwood.

50 The Official Opening of the Shire Hall, West Suffolk County Council, Wednesday, 16 October 1968, p6

6   The Swinging Sixties

The project at Bury St Edmunds represented the varied quality of McMorran & Whitby's output. Though the project was compromised by the client, the architects' own contributions were also found wanting. Encapsulated in one project, it was an apposite reflection of their often inconsistent output throughout the 1960s, which swung wildly from the sublime to the ridiculous. Between these extremes fell many projects for which the practice is less renowned, including The King's School in Chester, City of London Corporation housing at Holloway Road in north London, 100 Pall Mall, a church at Amersham and the bridge over the River Wye at Hereford.

As the decade started, McMorran & Whitby were heavily engaged upon a number of major projects and it is easy to overlook these smaller works, which helped to maintain a sizeable staff at 14 North Audley Street, as well as others to whom work was farmed out under the practice's name. These lesser-known works, slighter in size or less iconic in stature, which proliferated in the 1960s, represented a variety of projects that characterised the identity of 14 North Audley Street collectively, whereas the works of the previous decade were evidently from McMorran's hand. Among these jobs was the only religious building the practice ever built: Amersham Free Church, which McMorran received through his relationship with the City of London Corporation. The church's financial secretary, Eric Wilkins, had been on the City's housing committee when McMorran was assessor to the Golden Lane Housing Scheme, and invited McMorran to design the new church, which was opened on 30 September 1962.

14 North Audley Street, like any family residence, had its fair share of visitors (clients or otherwise) and, on occasions, lodgers, many of whom brought their own colour to the address and added to the melodrama. Given the prevailing atmosphere of busyness bordering on chaos, McMorran nicknamed the senior secretary, Betty Murray, 'Casabianca', after the fated ship in the poem by Felicia Hemans. She was forever the one left standing 'on the burning deck, whence all but he had fled …'. Sydney Toy, the architectural historian and expert on fortifications, was a friend of Farquharson and McMorran and would frequently be in the office, storing his possessions in the basement. Raymond Cochrane, born Rosemary, was another such character. Being among the early pioneers to have undergone a sex change, Cochrane later married and lived in the village of Guiting Power in the Cotswolds with his wife Sally. His relationship with 14 North Audley Street involved many jobs over several decades for the design and renovation of buildings in the village.

These jobs were a far cry from the two projects for which McMorran & Whitby would be most renowned: City Police Station in Wood Street and the extension to the Central Criminal Court in Old Bailey. These commissions for the City of London

Opposite: Central Criminal Court, Old Bailey, 1960–72

Amersham Free Church, 1960–2

Sketch design (interior and exterior) for
Amersham Free Church

Greyfriars Bridge, Hereford, 1954–58

Corporation appeared at the beginning of the 1960s and dominated the practice's output thereafter. Distinct within the oeuvre of the practice for their bold elevations sculpted from Portland stone rather than brick, their evolution can be traced back to a design in 1956 by McMorran for an office building on Gloucester's Westgate Street. It is uncertain whether this proposal was to be faced in brick or stone, but the concept drawing, by the Dorking-based architectural illustrator Arthur Shearing, suggests a surface possessing the evenness of stone with fittingly simple lines of unadorned fenestration. It synthesises McMorran's earlier works and point towards several of his later designs: his flats at Parkhill Road in Hampstead can be seen in the orderly lines of windows spanning a broad façade, and the shallow balconies with their metal railings hark back to the police section house in Mare Street in Hackney. However, it is forward, not back, that this proposal predominantly points. The combination of rectangular and segmental-arched windows and their changing rhythms between the ground and upper floors were to emerge at Exeter, Nottingham and Bury St Edmunds, and the comparatively austere elevation and shallow-pitched slate roof suggest a character yet to materialise.

This combination of ideas appeared somewhat prematurely in McMorran's design for 100 Pall Mall, the site of the former Carlton Club, which was destroyed during the war and which stands next to Sir Charles Barry's Reform Club. Planning permission was granted in 1957 for offices on this prominent West End location then owned by Rudolph Palumbo. The architects Duke & Simpson were responsible for the design of the proposed six-storey office building, with McMorran acting as consulting architect for the exterior, perhaps because a 'traditional style' was sought. The following year, McMorran's proposed façade, drawn by his assistant David Ancill, was exhibited at the Royal Academy Summer Exhibition.

The façade comprises a sheer wall of Portland stone largely stripped of detailing or ornamentation, leaving only the subtly changing rhythm of the windows cut through the pale stone to present the sober identity of the block to the street. The fenestration defines the five portions of the façade, which are revealed most noticeably along the roofline. The symmetrical composition forms the main body of the building, defined by the principal entrance contained within a familiar scheme of three segmental-arched openings at street level and flanked by two tall windows. The centrepiece of five windows extends for five floors to the entablature, above which it steps back from the façade. This arrangement is flanked by two wings, each two windows in width, that rise an extra two floors. Outside these wings, completing the five portions, are two narrower wings of equal height to the central portion of the building, which help to buffer the building from its neighbours in a similar manner to that employed by McMorran at Hammersmith Police Station. There are resonances, too, with Hackney in its carved niches, shallow balconies and strongly defined storeys and roofline – but it is in its broad surface of stone that this façade is most illuminating, as this is what McMorran ultimately took to Wood Street and the Old Bailey. It was over 100 Pall Mall that the writer of his obituary in *The Times* chose to criticise McMorran for 'his brand of period reminiscence', invoking a defence from his friend John Betjeman, who thought

100 Pall Mall, 1957–62

this a 'solid, three-dimensional composition of stone in a stone street of Renaissance character [that] depends for effect on proportion rather than detail'.[1]

Two years after McMorran's design appeared at the RA, another scheme, this time drawn by McMorran and Nigel Cowell 'at the request of the late Sir Robert Peel', was displayed in the Summer Exhibition of 1960 and titled 'Study of a Façade'.[2] The design was the first published incarnation of what would become the City Police Headquarters on Wood Street, or Barbican Block G as it was known to City planners. The reviewer for the *Builder*, the Canterbury architect Robert Paine, acknowledged this proposal as a 'highly competent drawing' and, in a short but quite profound observation, suggested 'Mr [Raymond] Erith should look out'.[3] A review of the Royal Academy Exhibition for 1965, which featured Sydney Evans's superb elevation of the City Police Station in Wood Street, concluded that 'in the realm of draughtsmanship there is no doubt that the "Old Master" school of architects put all else to shame'.[4]

Erith and McMorran were professional allies and shared certain architectural sympathies, though Erith was not a political animal and avoided confrontation where McMorran was happy to wade in up to his neck and beyond. The two shared prominent positions at the RA, where McMorran had been an associate since 1955. His primary backer was E. Vincent Harris, seconded by A. E. Richardson, Charles Cundall, Arnold Mason, Maurice Lambert, Sir Edward Maufe, Louis de Soissons and Sir Giles Gilbert Scott, a good friend of Farquharson. McMorran became a Royal Academician in 1962, when as his diploma work he hurriedly submitted a drawing from a decade earlier titled 'Group of Estate Cottages, Buckinghamshire'. This scheme, on the high street in West Wycombe, had likely been commissioned by the Dashwoods, who then owned the village, but it was never built and the slightly ill-fitting village hall was built in its place. This steady path, which also included increasing involvement at the RIBA, the election to Master of the Art Workers Guild in 1956 and membership of various exclusive clubs including the Athenæum (1962) and the influential Foreign Architectural Book Society, was one that saw McMorran being gradually accepted into the Establishment, that most British of constructs, which he so loved to hate yet whose draw he found irresistible. Having been on the RA Diners' Club Committee and the RA Finance Committee, McMorran was swiftly sucked into the complex politics of the Academy, a situation he doubtless relished and surely did little to resist. Harris, one of McMorran's chief allies in these circles, had been Treasurer there, but when McMorran joined the Finance Committee, the Treasurer was Basil Spence, the Secretary was Humphrey Brooke and the President was the sculptor Sir Charles Wheeler. Bad blood between McMorran and Spence went back years and was irredeemable. It might have started with the competition to design the new Coventry Cathedral, which Spence won in 1951. McMorran submitted a curiously modern scheme that had a large, circular central body, punctured by a series of round windows, sitting on a rectangular mass of stone dissected by glass volumes cut into its surface. Harris wrote to McMorran shortly after the result was announced to console him: 'You have no cause to worry you are going to come out all right later on for you possess both the persistence and ability', reassuring him that 'he [had] been in a similar situation many times and my dominant feeling has been pity for the asses who preferred some one else to me'.[5]

McMorran and Spence frequently came head to head. At the RIBA, where Spence was President from 1958 to 1960, and where McMorran had exerted influence as Honorary Secretary and chairman of various committees and boards (see Appendix 2 for full list), they often had bitter altercations. McMorran 'always maintained an individual point of view and would never compromise with principle', which 'sometimes caused him to seem at odds with his colleagues and contemporaries; but his friends valued him all the more for his sincerity'.[6] Not being able to 'aspire to batter the RIBA from without', McMorran was one of a few who had 'been carrying on a sapping operation from within'.[7] He was frequently critical of the then 'parlous state of the Institute's finances' and 'quietly and remorselessly rubbed their nose in unpalatable financial fact'.[8] Spence called for McMorran's resignation following his appearance on a programme televised by Granada TV called *Under Fire*, in which he and David Booth were quizzed by angry young architects from an audience in Manchester. McMorran's comments, which he frequently voiced elsewhere, suggesting the need to hold more competitions so that young architects could get

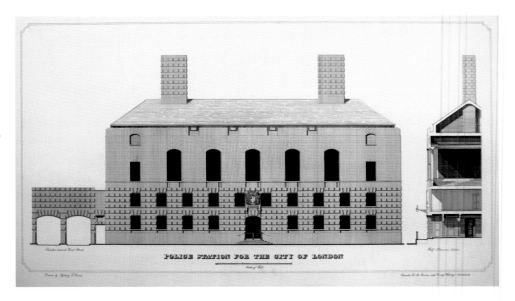

Elevation of Wood Street Police Station drawn by Sydney Evans, 1965

their foot on the ladder, apparently aroused consternation from Spence, who claimed McMorran was being disloyal to the RIBA. McMorran was used to this, though, as for much of the 1950s he was convinced that '"they" had been plotting to get rid of' him and his allies.[9]

However, it was at the RA in 1964, when Spence was Treasurer, that the showdown between him and McMorran ultimately took place. In McMorran's capacity as a council member of the RA and in his position on the Finance Committee, he chose to voice his concerns that 'the Academy's financial affairs were unsatisfactory'.[10] These concerns eventually caused 'very unfortunate repercussions'.[11] Spence regarded McMorran's remarks 'as implying criticism of himself [to which] he had reacted with extreme displeasure' and issued his resignation.[12] McMorran claimed 'he had not intended to attack the Treasurer personally but he had been concerned with the present system of control of expenditure and that other Members of the Finance Committee shared this concern'.[13] Spence was invited to reconsider his resignation, since the council unanimously agreed these concerns were of the 'system generally and not [about] the Treasurer', but it was too late; the die had been cast.[14]

A fellow member of the finance committee, Sir James Gunn, was appointed Treasurer in place of Spence, but he died shortly after his election and so, on 20 January 1965, McMorran was appointed the new Treasurer. Although Sir Charles Wheeler at once wrote to him stating 'I look forward to many occasions on which we shall have to consult and work together for the honour and glory of our Academy', this proved impossible.[15] The infamously sour politics at the RA got the better of everyone and the 'painful clash of

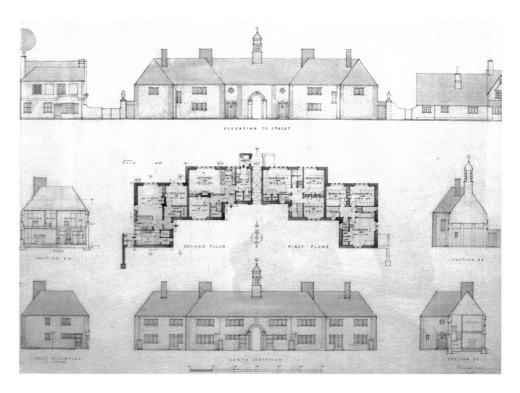

'Group of Estate Cottages, Buckinghamshire' – McMorran's Diploma work for the RA drawn in 1950

Sketch of McMorran's proposal for Coventry Cathedral, 1951

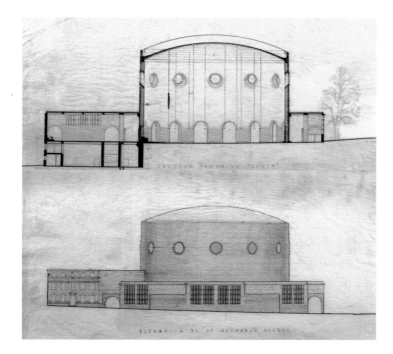

McMorran's proposal
for Coventry Cathedral,
1951

wills and a regrettable nuisance' caused McMorran to tender his resignation on 23 March 1965, though he officially remained in his post until his death in August.[16] The whole sorry episode profoundly upset McMorran. His obituary observed that 'it would have been a disappointment to him that he has not been spared to carry through the financial reforms needed by that ancient but somewhat creaking institution'.[17]

City Police Station, Wood Street

At the same time that this miserable incident was unfolding, McMorran was in the process of achieving the greatest success of his lifetime. Just before he died, the scaffolding came off the Headquarters of the City Police in Wood Street, though it would not be formally opened for another year. In 1990, Gavin Stamp, columnist at the *Spectator*, noted that the year 1965 claimed the lives of both Le Corbusier and McMorran as well as seeing 'the completion of the latter's Police Station in Wood Street, one of the most imaginative modern classical buildings in the City of London'.[18] At the time, even the *Architects' Journal* had to bow in the presence of this *tour de force* and concede to write about it, offering 'rather more than faint praise': 'In younger angrier days, Astragal [the pseudonymous author of the gossip column, written collectively but often containing the words of Sir Hugh Casson] would have attacked such a pretentious and phoney design, with anachronistic rusticated chimneys and mock load-bearing stonework. But McMorran was a sincere and devoted architect who cared passionately about what he was doing. So, crazy though it is, this police station is in another class from commercial trash nearby.'[19] Astragal was described by Erith as a 'silly little man', and McMorran had long since learned to ignore his whining from the wings.[20] Astragal's rare encomium after McMorran's death was clouded by his inability to make an objective analysis of a building that was contemporarily described as being 'generally distinguished in both form and detail, refusing to compromise with its environment [and] because of this its reputation may well outlast that of its less excellent neighbours'.[21] Less than two decades later, it was described in Jones and Woodward's *A Guide to the Architecture of London* as 'a very important building ... a very strong composition ... cool and abstracted'.[22]

More fervid even than Astragal, the architectural writer and critic Ian Nairn was unable to restrain his ire when writing in the *Observer* about the new building shortly after it was opened in 1966. He cynically accused McMorran of removing two Wren churches in the process of building this police station, an accusation he doubtless knew would rankle with an architect who championed the cause of preservation (had he still been alive to relish the challenge of being rankled).[23] The churches that Nairn was referring to were those of St Mary the Virgin, Aldermanbury, to the rear of the proposed police station, and St Albans, whose tower still stands as a private residence in front of it. Both structures were destroyed by the Luftwaffe during the Blitz, after which the Bishop's Commission decided that the latter be 'abandoned as no longer required' since it was deemed 'of only secondary Architectural interest'.[24] (The remains

City Police Station, Wood Street, shortly after completion in 1966

City Police Station, Wood Street, London, completed in 1966

of St Mary Aldermanbury were re-erected in 1965–9 at Westminster College, Fulton, Missouri.) Nevertheless, it was a point that Nairn had pursued blindly for years, causing the City Engineer to explain to McMorran that 'after a long municipal life, one has learned to expect inaccuracy in comment, and to achieve a fairly pachyder-matous condition'.[25] If only McMorran could have! Nairn did have the magnanimity to acknowledge that McMorran was 'unlike most neo-Georgians and knew exactly what he was doing', but this was only providing a counter to his criticisms for the building's 'naughty rustication' and the 'ferocious explosion of stonework with creepy overtones' in the 12-storey tower.[26]

McMorran's friend, Brian Harvey, whom he met in the war and for whom he later designed a house in Altrincham, visited City Police Station as it emerged from its scaffolding in the early summer of 1965. This was just as McMorran was retreating from public life. After the war, Harvey had been Chief Inspector of Factories and had culti-vated a professional interest in factory buildings, including 19th-century multi-storey mills. At McMorran's invitation he had once delivered a paper at the RIBA on the early industrial architecture of Lancashire. McMorran himself believed that mills descended

Above: Early sketch by McMorran of City Police Station, Wood Street, 1961

Left: Sketch proposal for City Police Station, Wood Street

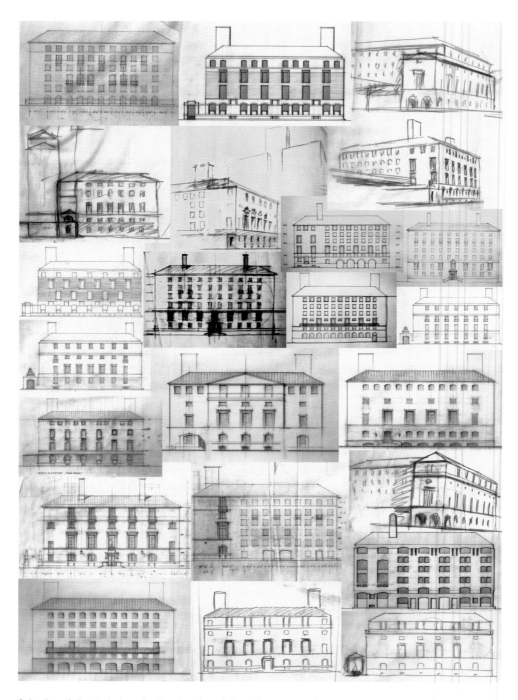

Selection of sketch designs for the elevation of Wood Street Police Station

from the 'sensible "Georgian" ways of building' and were 'the last works of traditional architecture in this country'.[27] Harvey viewed these structures as the early high-rises, and when McMorran was forced to add a tower to his City Police Station 'palazzo', which made him livid at the time, there is no question that Harvey's experience and knowledge of Britain's early industrial mills influenced the design (see page 138) and so too would the book *The Functional Tradition in Early Industrial Buildings*, which McMorran admired greatly but was written by another of his nemeses, J. M. Richards. In a covering letter to McMorran accompanying a set of small photographs of the building under construction, Harvey poignantly states: 'It is, if I may say so, I think the best I have seen of your work. It stands amidst its neighbours like a Wren church in a slum, an accusing monument of what a whole city might have looked like had there been any vision.'[28]

The City Police Station is an original masterpiece, a work of art that defines McMorran's philosophies succinctly. It is an Italianate composition harking back to his favourite architect, Michele Sanmicheli, yet is rooted firmly in Britain and in the 20th century. As McMorran said, 'It is what you *see* that matters.' Therefore, why should a nerve centre in the event of nuclear war not echo a palazzo? He rejected the notion that there could be such things as 'truth' and 'honesty' in art and architecture. Whose position was it to impose such moral judgements and why should it matter what materials an artist, sculptor or architect chose to create a piece of art? As McMorran wrote in 1959, 'so-called modern materials and methods are no more worthy than the old; and the principles of architecture – scale, proportion, and the rest – do not change and will be revenged on those who disregard them'.[29]

In a short documentary for the BBC, the illustrator Posy Simmonds studied City Police Station. 'When I first walked round this building, I thought this is really a joke, this is a police station that looks like an Italian palace, and then I later found out that that's precisely what McMorran intended, and apparently he laughed while he was designing it.'[30] He did so, not light-heartedly, but titillatingly. From the countless renditions he made for the façade, he at last produced a scheme that completely demonstrates his architectural ideals and the delight he took in drawing from the past in order to serve the needs of the future, such as his rusticated chimney stacks that house modern ventilation systems (see page 4) or the squash courts deep in the basement that convert into a nuclear bunker and nerve centre. He also could not resist small signature motifs and provocations that evidenced his reworking of classicism: no keystone separates the voussoirs on the gable walls of McMorran's tower, which meet affectionately, if inscrutably, in the centre of the windows facing Wood Street. Furthermore, each storey is inset from the floor below to create a tapering perspective that is most pleasing to the eye.

Between them, McMorran and Whitby were perfectly placed to achieve these objectives. Few British architects from this period could match McMorran's profound understanding of the art of architecture and his ability to handle an elevation while paying such exquisite attention to detail. His elevations were so often inscrutable: 'very reluctant to give anything away – a bit like his personality'.[31] Behind them, there were few who could manipulate space quite as brilliantly as Whitby. His mathematical mind could translate a plan into three dimensions to fit McMorran's disciplined elevations so that, inside and out, a building could come close to achieving, in the best examples of their work, perfection. At Wood Street, McMorran has produced multiple elevations behind which Whitby has grappled with extraordinary dexterity to place all the necessary demands of a modern police station. One of the practice's senior assistants, Ron Ringshall, was also heavily involved at Wood Street throughout the design and construction phases, before he moved on to the Greater London Council. Between them, they had to struggle with a brief that demanded not only the usual private offices and public spaces, but also squash courts, Turkish baths, cells, restaurants, stables, a tailor, a museum and accommodation for over 40 members of staff. That all this fitted so neatly behind McMorran's sublime exterior is testament to Whitby's ingenuity, and Wood Street represented the perfect flowering of their partnership.

Seen from the elevation facing Wood Street, McMorran's exterior of pure Portland stone brings together many elements from his previous work, most notably from Hammersmith Police Station. The symmetrical façade, substantial base, low roofline and visually dominant chimney stacks are obvious similarities, but at Wood Street, McMorran has placed the *piano nobile* on the top floor, standing above two shallower floors that have been given the visual strength to perform this function by the application of a band of sharp, almost abstracted, rustication that skirts the entire building.

The inner courtyard at City Police Station, Wood Street, showing Richard Rogers's 88 Wood Street (right) and Norman Foster's 100 Wood Street (left), behind

Every element of the façade has been carefully placed in relation to the whole, demonstrating once again McMorran's obsession with proportional arrangement. The rows of ten small windows on the ground and first floors define the position of the seven openings on the second floor. Tiny recesses below the bottom corners of the large second-floor windows serve as a link between the two principal portions of the building. On close inspection, it can be seen that it is in the proportional arrangement of these windows and the entrance that McMorran at last achieves perfection. It is that vision of a humane, well-mannered architecture, expert in the handling of its expressed materials, for which he had always been searching.

On the side elevation, facing Love Lane, McMorran adopts a different approach by dividing the *piano nobile* into two to create four storeys, while retaining the rustication on the lower two floors. On the ground floor, two large segmental-arched openings provide direct access into the courtyard where the stables are located. Not quite central to this elevation, a break in the rhythm of the fenestration offers the impression of a miniature tower that punctures the roofline with a pediment in which McMorran has placed five arched elements, three of which are ventilation shafts and two of which are empty niches. The curved heads of these details correspond with the segmental-arched windows along the top floor of the side and rear elevations. McMorran introduces these to the Wood Street façade in the form of single diminutive recesses that offer a visual association leading to the ultimate expression of this form in the five commanding windows that dominate the façade. At the foot, surrounding the entrance, are fine details in the moulded light brackets that also appear at Hammersmith and, before the current ramp was installed, iron railings for tying horses.

Rising above this elegant façade, and standing courteously to one side, is the tower containing offices and, on the top five floors, staff accommodation. McMorran was more than aware of the issues surrounding the construction of towers in the City. He was sympathetic to Renaissance styles being used on buildings up to 30 metres (100 feet) high, however 'extravagant and illogical' this might be, but he knew that for buildings any higher than this, such an expression becomes 'impossible or, if attempted, grotesque', resulting in the '"egg box" style which has been expounded *ad nauseam* in other great cities'. Unless the building can go high enough to acquire 'the dramatic effect of a tower, the architect in the City of London finds himself limited to a mere 150ft [and] has to make the worst of both worlds'.[32] McMorran highlighted an article by Sir William Holford, published in *The Times*, in which he suggested that such towers in areas like Golden Lane and Moorgate would not impact negatively on the City as they were sufficiently far from the sculptural qualities in and around St Paul's, but that until 'the new school of designers has evolved a better *average*' it behoves architects 'surely to build well within the traditional limits' closer to the cathedral.[33] However, at Wood Street McMorran has bequeathed to the City one of the world's most dignified classical high-rises – a slender slab of Portland stone pierced crisply with disciplined rows and columns of segmental-arched windows. One only need look around at the adjacent buildings to see that McMorran's tower possesses the vertical elegance of a campanile

Donald McMorran, painted shorty before he died, by Christopher Sanders RA

where others can only boast, brag and bluster as they extinguish the light and pleasure for the poor souls that occupy the streets below.

Nearly half a century on, the landscape around McMorran and Whitby's palazzo has almost completely changed, except for Wren's tower forming an island in the road. Despite interventions from many modern 'A-list' architects, the situation remains just as Brian Harvey described in 1965. While Nairn's blinkered opinion caused him to accuse McMorran of participating in the destruction of Wren's churches, today the building that took the place of St Mary Aldermanbury stands, as Harvey said it would, like a Wren church surrounded by a slum.

Harvey's letters and photographs were a kind gesture aimed at lightening the heart of a terminally ill man. From April 1965, McMorran never again worked at 14 North Audley Street. He was just about able to work on the design of a house at Fulmer for Ronald Edgley, which he could do from home. On 6 August 1965, McMorran died of cancer at his home in Dorking, aged 61. The impact upon his family, friends and colleagues was profound. 'That great man Donald McMorran,' John Betjeman wrote, 'I admired him as a person and as an architect.'[34] A recurring sentiment was that he was 'one of the few remaining real architects',[35] the last from a 'dwindling band of "sensible" architects'[36] and 'one of the few who really thought about his beloved art of architecture'.[37] He was, to some, 'one of the exceptional people one meets rarely in life',[38] and although his passing was a 'grievous loss to architecture',[39] 'his influence in architecture will certainly not die with him'.[40] The office felt they had 'lost the head of [their] family and nobody could ever replace him'.[41] The devotion that his colleagues held for him surprised even his widow. A senior assistant, Jim Peters, who had worked with McMorran since 1959, wrote: 'I am sure he never would have admitted it, but he was deeply admired for his integrity and strength of character. His was a strong and sure guiding hand, and this, with great personal charm, won our love and loyalty.'[42] But for a man who gave so much to his work in his lifetime, his legacy is perhaps best described by David Farquharson, the son of his mentor and former partner: 'His work has added immeasurably to the stature of the best of contemporary British architecture, and will live to commemorate him centuries after we are all gone.'[43]

With McMorran no longer at 14 Audley Street, the practice underwent a period of transformation and instability. Various senior assistants were offered partnerships, but some refused, while others left. Jim Peters became a partner on paper, but soon afterwards left the office, and it was not until 1969 that Norman Walker, who declined the offer of a partnership in 1965 and left for America, returned and accepted the advancement.

The practice still had a number of major projects under way, principally as a result of the good relationship McMorran had built with the Corporation of London. One of these was the two-phased Holloway Road Housing Estate in north-east London. The first phase was completed in the mid-1960s and comprised a large, dignified and well-

Holloway Road Housing Estate (first phase), Islington, London, 1959–65

McMorran House in Holloway Road Housing Estate, 1959–65

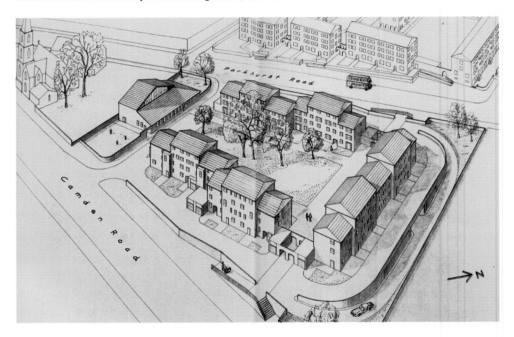

Sketch proposal for the second phase of Holloway Road Housing Estate, 1971, showing the first phase in the background

kempt scheme of three- and four-storey blocks composed, in a familiar configuration, around two courtyards. In the centre, between the courtyards, is McMorran House, whose miniature arcade distinguished it from the surrounding buildings, themselves united by linking screen walls pierced with round-arched gateways. The second phase was designed by Whitby and completed in the mid-1970s. It stands on the other side of

York Way Housing Estate, completed in 1969 (windows altered), showing the tower of Bunning's original Caledonian Road Market (far left), Islington, London, 1969

Holloway Road and is worked out around a central courtyard that shields the dwellings from the busy roads that run down both sides of the site. It bears little resemblance to the practice's signature style, but it was a pioneering scheme wherein a fifth of the residents were disabled and their specially designed flats were dispersed among the other residential units. This was an attempt by the architects and the client (the City Corporation in partnership with the John Grooms Association for the Disabled) to better integrate disabled people into communities. This demand had been made by the Conservative Party in their 1966 election manifesto, and it led to the Chronically Sick and Disabled Persons Act of 1970. Out of respect to its architect, who died before the project was completed, the scheme was named Whitby Court.

Another housing scheme for the City Corporation was York Way Housing Estate in Islington, completed in 1969. This is said to have been designed principally by Peters and is a far cry from the work McMorran produced, although he had accepted that the practice needed to adapt if it was to survive. This colossal scheme, comprising 3 eight-storey and 1 four-storey brick-faced slab blocks containing 275 flats and maisonettes, was situated on the site of the former Caledonian Road Market, designed by J. B. Bunning (1852–5). The redevelopment of the site called for the destruction of two Italianate hotels and two of four large public houses (the latter eventually all retained), while the central clock tower was preserved as the hub of the new layout.

The Central Criminal Court, Old Bailey

Although the workload in the practice slowly dwindled towards the end of the 1960s, there was one project that occupied much of Whitby's time and, arguably, stands as the greatest monument to him and McMorran. In the early 1960s, as McMorran laboured to arrive at a viable façade for City Police Station, the office produced reams and reams of sketches with different configurations of fenestration. Among these piles of papers, one stands out for bearing a more than a passing resemblance to the eventual elevation of the Central Criminal Court on Old Bailey.

This was the largest job the practice undertook in the City of London, and the last project that both partners would work on together. In 1960, the idea to extend the crowded Central Criminal Courts was first proposed. In November 1962, the City's Court of Common Council approved McMorran's initial designs for this extension, which only had a slender façade on Old Bailey, but in 1963 more land next to E. W. Mountford's original building (1902) was purchased, thereby permitting the very much larger façade that was eventually built. Since the new building had to retain the sense of scale and proportion of Mountford's main elevation, an 'awful lot of Old Bailey was fixed before McMorran died'.[44]

The Old Bailey façade is a tantalising glimpse of the heights McMorran & Whitby might have reached had both partners not died so relatively young. Despite his formidable ability, McMorran ultimately lacked the confidence to experiment with forms other than those with which he was brought up and which were part of his very being. How lucky, he would say of the Modernists, that they do not have to burden themselves with historical precedent. But for McMorran it was not about classicism or modernism: he was concerned with 'humanism', 'with buildings related to human beings – in an age in which human values and the human scale are at a discount'.[45] His bibles were *The Architecture of Humanism* by Geoffrey Scott and *Architectural Principles in the Age of Humanism* by Rudolph Wittkower.[46] The classical idiom happened to be the vocabulary McMorran used to articulate his artistic ambitions, which he believed should be concentrated entirely on serving the user. While this caused him to be largely ostracised by his peers, at Old Bailey, McMorran managed to liberate himself from his branding as a traditionalist. It was at home in Dorking, watched by his son Alexander, Kingston School of Art and Civic Design, (part of Kingston College of Art) that McMorran laboured over designs for the façade of the Central Criminal Court. In the face of persistent opposition by Modernists for sticking to his classical principles, the elder McMorran would repeatedly and rhetorically ask: 'Am I doing the right thing?' He was a great admirer of Dance's Newgate Prison which had stood on the site until demolished to make way for Mountford's building. Newgate itself was inspired by the famous prison fantasy drawings of Giovanni Battista Piranesi (1720–78). It was Alexander who suggested he might look to the work of Louis Kahn (1901–74) for further inspiration, and the result fronting Old Bailey is McMorran's response: a highly original composition sculpted in stone and demonstrative of the compressive architecture he championed. It was, as one critic wrote some years later, 'well ahead of its time in the abandonment

McMorran & Whitby's extension to the Central Criminal Court, 1960–72 showing the original building by Mountford (left), 1902

1970 illustration of the Central Criminal Court, Old Bailey, London, 1960–72 by Arthur Shearing

View of the rear of the Central Criminal Court,
Old Bailey, London, 1960–72

of Modernist conventions, not for the new vernacular, but for a far more coherent and radical style'.[47] The giant recessed segmental-arched window openings allow dramatic vertical strips of stone containing ventilating shafts to cascade down the façade and plunge from view in beautifully angled chamfers that drive into the wall above the four splendid low doorways, echoing but surpassing the sculptural qualities of Lutyens's Castle Drogo or Holden's Bristol Central Library. The whole effect is to emphasise the sheer, apparently suspended, mass above the 'formidable entrance'.[48] This is a structure that appears hewn, not built. It is primordial in unaffected magnificence, ushering visitors into a building of such startling originality that it is both peerless and ageless.

There was some debate as to whether the project could proceed after McMorran died, but it was eventually decided that the practice, with Whitby at the helm, could see it through to completion. While McMorran had been able to set the mould for the exterior, it was up to Whitby to mastermind the planning. The extension to the Central Criminal Court represents the acme of Whitby's extraordinary spatial faculty and is a reflection of his perfectionism. The original brief called for six courts to be housed inside this extension, but in 1966 this was increased to 12 in order to cope with the expansion of the London Administrative Area the year before. Anne Mallinson JP, the first Lay Magistrate to sit in the City of London Magistrates Courts, assisted the office to have the plans amended – this was achieved in ten days. Anne later became the Lord Mayor of Westminster. Not only did Whitby have to find a way to house 12 courts in a space originally intended for six, but he also had to accommodate this while respecting the typically complex circulatory problems posed by courts. He had to contend with the fact that the courts had to be separately accessed from the street by four different groups of users: judge and jury, barristers and witnesses, defendants, and the general public. The need for people to circulate around the building without ever coming into contact with anyone but members of their own group demanded an astonishing plan, which exists as a legacy of an exceptional talent.

The new building also had to dovetail with Mountford's so that the individual floor levels would be continued throughout the extension. This was further complicated by the topography of the site which not only slopes down Old Bailey to the south, making the ground floor entrance of McMorran & Whitby's extension one floor lower than Mountford's, but also rises from front to back. The latter change in level is the result of the building being positioned on the line of London's Roman wall inside of which centuries of development has caused the ground to be a storey higher than that outside the wall. The remains of the Roman wall, along with a collapsed portion of wall from Dance's

Interior lobby of the Central Criminal Court, completed in 1972

Lift lobby in the Central Criminal Court   Interior showing corridor through to Mountford's original building, 1902

George Whitby (left) and the Clerk of Works (right) at the Central Criminal Court

Newgate Prison, were uncovered during construction. Whitby insisted the Roman wall should remain in situ and it can be found in the plant room directly ahead of the entrance on the ground floor, Dance's Prison wall was re-erected and can be viewed through the judges' entrance at the rear. Interestingly, Whitby's solution of linking the plant rooms on the ground floor and roof through service ducts set proud on the building's façades was explained many years later to John Pringle (formerly of Michael Hopkins and Partners) by Whitby's son, Mark, and provided an inspiration for the distinctive ventilation shafts on Hopkins's Portcullis House opposite the Houses of Parliament.

Construction of the Central Criminal Court started in 1970, and the foundation stone was laid by the Lord Mayor, Sir Ian Bowater, on 4 May. Two years later, on 27 September 1972, the building was opened to the public. The architectural press had already made up its mind and continued its onslaught against the practice's output by disparaging the design as best it could. *Building Design* claimed it did 'little justice to architecture old or new',[49] while the *Architects' Journal* proposed that it looked like a penitentiary with its imagery suggesting 'abandon hope all ye who enter here'.[50] Both failed to see that humanity was permitted in the building by the very 'avoidance of any grand entrance',[51] befitting a building that Whitby believed would provide a 'more intimate, human and informal atmosphere'.[52] There is no doubt that the building possesses an 'austere elegance and dignity', but this surely suits a structure serving such a purpose.[53] The physical embodiment of a legal system that is supposed to uphold the very structure of a civilisation should not be a jocular whimsy. It is indeed a 'splendid fortress of the law',[54] as John Betjeman described it.

The building's £7.5 million price tag also attracted criticism. The internal walls everywhere were faced in travertine stone, floors in Broughton Moor slate, and the roof in Westmorland slate, which Whitby's eldest son, Richard, helped to lay. The quality of

Horace and Noël Farquharson on their 50th
wedding anniversary

finish and very careful attention to detail, as ever with McMorran & Whitby's work, were
superb – particularly in the joinery, which was said to have 'achieved a peak of excellence
which can hardly be rivalled elsewhere'.[55] The Lord Mayor's dining room was panelled
in London plane, which was very hard to find without shrapnel imbedded in it from the
Blitz. But a different type of explosive had a greater impact on the building shortly after
it was completed. On 8 March 1973, a massive IRA car bomb was detonated right outside
McMorran and Whitby's fortress. The cliff face of Portland stone survived almost without
a scratch, while the glass curtain walling of nearby modern buildings, such as 'that
dreadful building by Theo Birks on the opposite side of Old Bailey', was shattered.[56]

Only days before this atrocity, Whitby died at his home in Penn, Buckinghamshire,
aged 56. At his memorial service, the Poet Laureate, John Betjeman, delivered a poem he
wrote in tribute to the last work of 'that great architect':

> ... Behold the Law's new fortress, ramparting over the Bailey
> In cream-coloured clear-cut ashlar on grim granite foundations
> But like all good citizens, paying regard to its neighbours,
> Florid baroque on one side, plain commercial the other,
> This is your work, George Whitby, whose name to-day we remember;
> From Donald McMorran and Dance to Wren and Nicolas Hawksmoor,
> You stand in a long tradition; and we who are left salute you.[57]

Whitby's death signalled also the ultimate demise of the practice. In the mid-1970s,
after the death of the two principal partners, McMorran & Whitby lent their services
to Brian Colquhoun and Partners (the civil engineers) in partnership with Cable and
Wireless for a large and swift project to design the buildings for four airports in Sudan,
including Juba and Port Sudan. The designs comprised terminal buildings, VIP lounges,
and even a special terminal for passengers en route to Mecca for the Hajj. McMorran's

son Alexander, as a qualified architect, led a team of ten assistants, including two specially trained Sudanese students.

However, this commission was a special case and the practice, surviving in name only but with Norman Walker at its head, closed in 1982. It was a relatively muted end to an office born out of professional admiration and very many genuine friendships, from Farquharson to McMorran to Whitby. Though McMorran spent more of his life with Farquharson, he was closer in age to Whitby and clearly the two complemented one another admirably – McMorran the artist and Whitby the planner. McMorran believed there were three facets of good architecture: art, planning and building; or as Sir Henry Wotton put it, albeit in a different order, commodity, firmness and delight. McMorran provided the delight and Whitby the commodity. Although the practice was officially divided 60/40, their relationship was based on mutual respect and friendship. Both were perfectionists, in the true sense of the word, and they shared a fanatical commitment to their work, the architecture always coming 'first, second and third'.[58] Between them, they had built not only a large and productive practice but also a happy one. A Chinese assistant, Robert Yap, described his time at 14 North Audley Street as the happiest days of his life.

Within the space of just a few years, the deaths of McMorran (1965), Farquharson (1966), Harris (1971), Whitby (1973) and finally McMorran's friend Erith (1973) saw the severance of the thin thread of classicism in later 20th-century British architecture. John Brandon-Jones provided a fitting testimony to this delicate strand of architecture when he wrote:

McMorran & Whitby were among the leaders of the small band of architects who have demonstrated the possibility of applying classical principles in the design of large modern buildings. Over and over again, they were able to show that the traditional formulae were capable of infinite variety and also that, for many purposes, traditional materials and craftsmanship could still compete successfully with system building from the economic as well as from the aesthetic point of view ... their work will remain a challenge and an inspiration to many younger architects, disillusioned by mass production and by the aridity of so much contemporary design.[59]

Notes

1   Unpublished letter from John Betjeman to *The Times*, 10 August 1965.
2   Robert Paine, 'Academy Architecture – 1960', *Builder*, 6 May 1960, p866.
3   ibid.
4   *Builder*, 7 May 1965, p994
5   Letter from E. Vincent Harris to McMorran, undated; courtesy of the McMorran family archive.
6   Letter from Arthur Llewellyn-Smith to Margaret McMorran, 10 August 1965; courtesy of the McMorran family archive.
7   Letter from McMorran to Albert Richardson, 6 July 1954; courtesy of the McMorran family archive.
8   *Builder*, 13 August 1965, p331.
9   Letter from McMorran to Albert Richardson, 6 July 1954; courtesy of the McMorran family archive.
10 McMorran, Royal Academy Minutes, 8th Council meeting, 13 July 1964.
11 Wheeler, Royal Academy Minutes, 12th Council meeting, 27 October 1964.

12 Spence, Royal Academy Minutes, 12th Council meeting, 27 October 1964.

13 McMorran, Royal Academy Minutes, 12th Council meeting, 27 October 1964.

14 Royal Academy Minutes, 12th Council meeting, 27 October 1964.

15 Letter from Charles Wheeler to McMorran, 22 January 1965; courtesy of the McMorran family archive.

16 Letter from Charles Wheeler to Margaret McMorran, Easter Day 1965; courtesy of the McMorran family archive.

17 *Builder*, 13 August 1965, p331.

18 *Spectator*, 13 January 1990, p9.

19 *Architects' Journal*, 6 July 1966, p6.

20 Letter from Raymond Erith to McMorran, 12 February 1955; courtesy of the McMorran family archive.

21 *Financial Times*, 30 June 1966.

22 Edward Jones and Christopher Woodward, *A Guide to the Architecture of London*, London, Weidenfeld and Nicholson, 1983, p291; see also Jonathan Meades, 'City guidelines', in *Architects' Journal*, 1 June 1983, p41.

23 McMorran was Joint Secretary of the Dorking and Leith Hill District Preservation Society, the Chairman of which was the composer Ralph Vaughan Williams.

24 Extract from the report by the Bishop's Commission, quoted in a letter from the City Engineer to Donald McMorran, 13 April 1960.

25 Letter from the City Engineer to Donald McMorran, 13 April 1960; courtesy of the McMorran family archive.

26 Ian Nairn, 'Architecture Against Crime', *Observer*, 14 August 1966.

27 McMorran, 'The Value of Design in Rural Buildings', lecture, undated.

28 Letter from Brian Harvey to Donald McMorran, 4 April 1965; courtesy of the McMorran family archive.

29 McMorran, Letter to *The Times*, 20 November 1959.

30 Posy Simmonds, *Building Sights, Designs of the Times*, Directed by Francesca Joseph, BBC 2, 8.50 p.m., 17 June 1996.

31 Letter from William McMorran to Gavin Stamp, 28 January 1992; courtesy of Gavin Stamp.

32 McMorran, Letter to *The Times*, 27 January 1954.

33 Sir William Holford, 'Reflections on the City Skyline', *The Times*, 19 June 1953.

34 Letter from John Betjeman to Margaret McMorran, 10 August 1965; courtesy of the McMorran family archive.

35 Letter from Francis Broadbent to Margaret McMorran, 9 August 1965; courtesy of the McMorran family archive.

36 Letter from Henry Medd to Margaret McMorran, 11 August 1965; courtesy of the McMorran family archive.

37 Letter from W. A. Eden to Margaret McMorran, 9 August 1965; courtesy of the McMorran family archive.

38 Letter from Brian O'Rorke to Margaret McMorran, 12 August 1965; courtesy of the McMorran family archive.

39 Letter from Godfrey Samuel to Margaret McMorran, 15 August 1965; courtesy of the McMorran family archive.

40 Letter from Ian Lesley to Margaret McMorran, 8 August 1965; courtesy of the McMorran family archive.

41 Letter from Irene (Betty) Smallwood to Margaret McMorran, 9 August 1965; courtesy of the McMorran family archive.

42 Letter from James Peters to Margaret McMorran, 7 August 1965; courtesy of the McMorran family archive.

43 Letter from David Farquharson to Margaret McMorran, 12 August 1965; courtesy of the McMorran family archive.

44 Charmian Smith (formerly Whitby), interview with author, 9 September 2008.

45 Raymond Cochrane, in a letter to Margaret McMorran, 29 October 1965; courtesy of the McMorran family archive.

46 Geoffrey Scott, *The Architecture of Humanism*, London, Constable, 1914, and Rudolph Wittkower, *Architectural Principles in the Age of Humanism*, London, Alex Tiranti, 1952.

47 Brian Appleyard, 'From God's House to Bauhaus and Back Again', *The Times*, 20–26 November 1982.

48 Letter from John Betjeman to Charmian Whitby, 14 March 1973; courtesy of the Whitby family archive.

49 *Building Design*, 8 September 1972, p7.

50 *Architects' Journal*, 6 September 1972, p516.

51 Appleyard, *op. cit.*

52 *The Times*, 1 September 1972.

53 *The Times*, 3 March 1973.

54 Letter from John Betjeman to Charmian Whitby, 14 March 1973; courtesy of the Whitby family archive.

55 *Building*, 8 September 1972, p80.

56 ibid.

57 Delivered by John Betjeman at George Whitby's memorial service, St Mary Woolnoth, 29 March 1973.

58 Clare Sims, interview with Charmian Smith (formerly Whitby), undated.

59 *The Times*, 3 March 1973.

7   McMorran & Whitby's Legacy

Although the personalities that contributed to the best designs emanating from 14 North Audley Street are no longer alive, their legacy is more pertinent today than ever since their work is of the rare type that improves with age. It lives on in their buildings and in their writings, though neither has hardly been studied. This is partly because their work was largely ignored at the time, but also partly because it has never really been understood. As McMorran's youngest architect son, William, noted: 'When the work was bad it was terribly dismal, but when it was good it was such an extraordinary demonstration of how to pursue an architecture of this form, that few if any can understand what is going on.'[1]

Art, planning and construction: these are what defined architecture for McMorran and they relied completely on an effective relationship between the architect, the builder and the client. It was this conviction and his devotion to the art of building that caused him to be elected Master of the Art Workers Guild. He 'could not help associating the poor design of so much of our building today with the purely modern notion that architecture could be taught in schools, as a kind of abstraction, without tradition, and apart from its practice as an essential part of the building industry'.[2] Few things in the professional sphere concerned him more than the direction in which architectural education was heading. 'The real danger of this situation is that architects are putting themselves in an ivory tower, and I am afraid they may be losing their position of master builders', he said in one lecture, suggesting that architects would soon become 'mere "cosmeticians" for the building industry [which] would be a sad thing for the ancient art of architecture'.[3]

But these failings were, to McMorran, symptomatic of a wider problem in the profession that was being perpetuated by a professional press constantly peddling the notion of 'style for the sake of style'.[4] Although McMorran and Whitby faced their fair share of criticism in the press, they were dispassionate about the reasons for this. McMorran believed Britain was unique in having weekly professional papers, the consequence of which was that 'our journalists have no time to think. Their very existence depends on their advertisements and their advertisements depend on circulation. To keep up their circulation in the glossy modern world they must at all costs be exciting. So they are engaged in a feverish and never ending search for novel and titillating material.'[5] Raymond Erith, also often vilified for the traditional character of his work, shared this view, writing to McMorran in 1955 complaining that 'the real problem is not inside the RIBA. It is in the people who dish out the ideas and use this control of the press to intimidate the profession into acceptance. I don't believe half the Modernists have got their heart and soul in what the *Architectural Review* calls contemporary architecture: a lot of them are really quite good architects. If you can persuade a few of them out of their mood of defeatism things would soon look different … All that matters is that they should be momentarily eye-catching.'[6]

The popular ephemeral take on architecture rankled McMorran and Whitby because it represented the antithesis of their work. Because they rejected faddishness and fashion, they were pigeon-holed as being 'traditional', their plans interpreted as expressing 'the dull axiality of fag-end classicism'[7] carried out by 'arch-conservative' architects.[8] However, not all commentators misunderstood. H. A. N. Brockman of the *Financial Times* wrote, in 1964, of the practice's work as the 'logical use of mainly traditional materials, to produce a comfortable and acceptable environment for those who use their buildings. In both these categories fashionable trends are ignored and design is pursued as the expression of an individual conviction. The criterion to be applied to their work for its proper evaluation is that of intellectual and artistic integrity.'[9] Perhaps the best rebuttal of the media's representation of McMorran was that written by the architect and teacher William A. Eden in response to McMorran's obituary in *The Times*:

> *Your generous obituary of Donald McMorran suggests that his sympathies in architecture lay with the previous generation. Perhaps you will allow me, as one who enjoyed many a lively discussion with him on the subject of modern architecture, to say that he did not see it that way. Nobody was more aware than he of the need to come to terms with the modern world. He believed that an architect is the servant of his clients, and so in his work he strove, first and foremost, to achieve efficient planning and good building; but he believed also that these were not enough to make a building worthy of the name of architecture which, for him, was pre-eminently a matter of humane proportions. In his search for a means of humanizing the monster buildings demanded by our present society his mind ranged widely and he had the humility to accept what appeared to him to be a fruitful idea whatever its source … Perhaps he did not always succeed in his object; but he never capitulated.*[10]

Art, planning and construction, where art is employed as the humanising element in an increasingly inhuman world: this is why it is *not* a surprise, despite what so many subsequent commentators have said, to see McMorran, in his capacity as assessor to the Golden Lane Estate in 1952, award the project to Geoffry Powell (later of Chamberlin, Powell and Bon). McMorran saw that the design was exceptionally well planned and believed his proposal was a genuine stroke of genius. Powell in turn acknowledged McMorran's kindness in finishing his cross-hatching when he handed in his entry uncompleted.[11] How curious it is to wonder what might have happened to London's famous Barbican had McMorran not enthused about this young and inexperienced talent. He was not against tower blocks: he just believed they could be 'put into good effect, in isolated cases'. 'It is important to consider', he said in a letter to *The Times*, 'what the result will be if this type of development is generally applied to a compact neighbourhood such as the City of London.'[12] If developers could be assisted to limit their demands on space and light (which would allow the City to remain a genial place) then 'leave St. Paul's and the church towers behind, make the sky the limit, and enjoy the different pleasures offered by twentieth-century architecture and planning. But do not expect compromise to produce anything but dreary mediocrity.'[13] These are not the words of an arch-conservative.

Humanity in architecture was essential to McMorran, with his broad view of history. 'The worst buildings of today', he said in a lecture in 1960, 'are certainly the worst in human history. The only hope is in a patient rediscovery of the humanist values.'[14] Though he was not a man of music, he readily accepted theoretical parallels with architecture and acknowledged these words penned by Hindemith in *A Composer's World*: 'the durable values of music are not forgotten; they are as alive as they were thousands of years ago, and we as musicians can do nothing better than to accept them as the guiding principles of our work.'[15] In deference to these enduring principles, McMorran believed that architects must look only to 'compressive structures', as they had since time immemorial.[16] 'All the great architecture of the past was based on the principle of compression only … a building cannot be wholly in tension.'[17] He understood that tensile elements were inevitable but should not be allowed to 'destroy the aesthetic significance of the building', a point he knew to be heretical in the 20th century.[18] Hence, materials like reinforced concrete, in which tension and compression are combined, are in McMorran's eyes, 'almost certainly unintelligible and therefore confusing and unpleasing (except in very simple structures)'. As for the Modernists who felt they knew only too well the absurdity of this heresy, McMorran suggested they need look only as far as their leader Le Corbusier, who 'in his later work has confounded his followers by turning from "bony" structures to "fat" ones like the chapel at Ronchamp which has the visual character of the old compressive architecture'.

It is often suggested that this humanistic quality in McMorran & Whitby's work is influenced by Scandinavian classical tradition. This proposition may have descended from an article by H. S. Goodhart-Rendel, in which he paid a compliment to Hammersmith Police Station by saying: 'I do not know the name of its designer, but I think it improbable that he was a Dane, I think it more likely that he was a sensitive English artist who, finding no civilized idiom in his own country, attached himself spiritually to the congenial school of modern Copenhagen.'[19] Although it is tempting to draw similarities between Scandinavian design and McMorran's work, especially with examples such as Kampmann's Police Headquarters in Copenhagen (1925), the former did not seek inspiration from Scandinavia, though he was very aware of its architecture, as he was of that of all countries and all epochs. The evolution of his style, which was seen to 'continue and to develop and adapt the English classical tradition to meet new and ever-changing building requirements', was influenced to a far greater degree by Britain's recent history, back through Harris, Lutyens and Soane to Renaissance Italy and, in particular, his idol, Michele Sanmicheli.[20]

The Renaissance architects were, to McMorran & Whitby, the true 'Modernists'. They were willing to embrace new materials and building types, but, unlike 20th-century Modernists, they 'accepted the experience of the building crafts and were glad to learn from it [and] made no claim to be original and inspired designers'.[21] In the modern era, the complete censure of tradition for its own sake – regardless of its profundity, regardless of the experience it encapsulates and regardless of the lessons it might teach – is, if allowed to take root, a measure of ignorance akin to that of Mao's Cultural Revolution or of Hitler's Germany. As the architectural correspondent in the *Financial Times* wrote in 1964, in the context of McMorran's Devon County Hall: 'it is easy for the devoted experimentalist in both aesthetics and technology to dismiss [their approach] as an unnecessary indulgence in the language of a dead past [but on] the other hand it cannot be ignored at a time when the technical revolution, which has succeeded substantially, has nevertheless failed so far to formulate a visual language or order which is readily understandable by those to whom it must ultimately and readily appeal.'[22] So it was, then, that 'Donald, with his exquisite sense of proportion in the humane tradition, was too early and too late for the current trend.'[23] McMorran knew his principled stand would bring him into conflict with those who did not share his views on architecture, and the price he paid was the same as those who preceded him in history: public hostility, professional exclusion and ill health.

However, time has vindicated McMorran's and Whitby's staunch convictions and enhanced their work – just as they intended and anticipated. Although 'traditionalism' remains an unshakeable label possessing negative undertones, they were a practice that 'stepped effortlessly beyond modernism without the struggles and indecision which have characterized the same step among others' – no mean feat in an age of architectural sectarianism.[24] Only when their work can be viewed in the broader timescales that dispense with the 'feverish succession of "-isms"' will they be judged fairly.[25] McMorran and Whitby were professionals seeking only the essence of their chosen art. This essence may come to be appreciated as ultimately more enduring than the vast output of their 20th-century contemporaries. Although it might never be truly timeless, it will be appreciated throughout time.

Notes

1   Letter from William McMorran to Gavin Stamp, 28 January 1992; courtesy of Gavin Stamp.
2   Paper given by McMorran at the RIBA Conference on Building Training, January 1956.
3   Donald McMorran, 'The Education of the Architect', lecture, undated, p10.
4   ibid., p9.
5   ibid., p10.
6   Letter from Raymond Erith to McMorran, 12 February 1955; courtesy of the McMorran family archive.
7   Lionel Brett, quoted in Fawcett and Jackson, *op. cit.*, p62.
8   Fawcett and Jackson, ibid., p95.
9   Brockman, *op. cit.*
10   Letter to *The Times*, 14 August 1965.
11   Geoffry Powell, 6 January 1999, to Elain Harwood.
12   McMorran, Letter to *The Times*, 4 June 1953.
13   McMorran, Letter to *The Times*, 27 January 1954.
14   McMorran, Draft Lecture Notes for 'Architecture in 1960', lecture, October 1960.

15   Paul Hindemath, *A Composer's World: Horizons and Limitations*, Havard University Press, Cambridge, 1952, p13.

16   ibid.

17   ibid.

18   ibid.

19   Goodhart-Rendel, *op. cit.*

20   Letter from John Brandon-Jones to Margaret McMorran, 9 August 1965; courtesy of the McMorran family archive.

21   McMorran, 'The Value of Design in Rural Buildings', lecture, undated.

22   Brockman, *op. cit.*

23   Raymond Cochrane in a letter to Margaret McMorran, 29 October 1965; courtesy of the McMorran family archive.

24   Appleyard, *op. cit.*

25   McMorran, Draft Lecture Notes for 'Architecture in 1960', lecture, October 1960.

1940

Estate Plan, RIBA Competition
for 'Industrial Housing in Wartime,'
Farquharson & McMorran
(£10 prize)

1950

Hunstanton Secondary School,
Hunstanton, Norfolk, George Whitby
(Competition, third place)
Client: Norfolk County Council
Builder, 12 May 1950, pp642–4

1950

Group of Cottages, High Street,
West Wycombe, Buckinghamshire,
Donald McMorran
Client: West Wycombe Estate
The Times, 14 April, 1944
Exhibited RA 1962

1951

Coventry Cathedral, Donald McMorran
(Competition, unplaced)

1955–6

Offices, Westgate Street, Gloucester,
Gloucestershire, Donald McMorran
Architect and Building News, 17 May 1956,
p523
Builder, 27 July 1956, p146

1958

National Gallery extension, London,
Donald McMorran
Client: Samuel Sebba

1959

St Paul's Choir School, City of London,
Donald McMorran with Seely & Paget
Client: Dean and Chapter of St Paul's
Builder, 6 April 1962, pp698–9

1961

**Woking Urban District Council Civic
Buildings**, Surrey, McMorran & Whitby
Client: Woking UDC

1964

Tonbridge Civic Centre, Kent,
Donald McMorran (unplaced)
Client: Tonbridge UDC
Builder, 24 January 1964, p175

c.1970

Port of London Authority Building,
Tower Hill, London, George Whitby
(Collaboration with building contractors,
Mowlem)
Client: Port of London Authority

Published Articles and Reports

'Use of outside architects by architects'
firms', *Architects' Journal* Info Library, 12
March 1959
'Report of the Architectural Education
Joint Committee on the Training and
Qualification for Associate Membership
of the Royal Institute of British Architects'
(otherwise known as the 'McMorran
Report'), RIBA, 1955
Architects' Journal, 10 February 1955,
pp183 and 195
Builder, 3 February 1961, p213
Builder, 9 November 1962, p913

Obituary: Donald McMorran

We announce with deep regret the death, which took place at Dorking on 6 August, of Mr. Donald McMorran, RA, FSA, FRIBA, Treasurer of the Royal Academy and senior partner in the firm of McMorran & Whitby, of North Audley-street, W1. He was 61.

Donald Hanks McMorran, born in 1904 and educated at Harrow County School, served his articles with Horace Farquharson and from 1927–35 was one of a brilliant group of assistants, which included the late E. Berry Webber and Mr. Arthur Bailey, that worked in the office of E. Vincent Harris. In 1935 he won the competition for York civic offices and rejoined Mr. Farquharson, this time as partner. Together they carried out many important buildings, two of which – the Blackheath-road police section house (1946) and the LCC open-air school, Bow-road, E3 (1952) – won the London Architecture Medal award of the RIBA. Other buildings for which he was responsible, in some cases with his partners, were Hammersmith police station; the police section house, Greenwich; housing estates at Hampstead, Poplar, Sydenham, Islington, Richmond and Dorking; schools at Poplar, Crigglestone, Harlow and Wakefield; The King's School, Chester; Lenton and Cripps halls and the social science and education departments, Nottingham University; reconstruction of the St. Stephen's Club, Queen Anne's-gate; county library and police station, Bury St. Edmunds; Devon County Hall, Exeter; and Crosby Merchant Taylors School hall. Buildings at present under construction include the new City police station, extensions to the Central Criminal Court, and West Suffolk shire hall extensions. He was also consultant for the Folkestone civic centre and the new Wye bridge at Hereford.

McMorran did much valuable and unobtrusive work for the interests of the profession. He was hon. secretary of the RIBA Board of Architectural Education, 1952–54 and as such was chairman of a report on architectural education the value of which is only now being recognised. His sound knowledge of architectural practice and of construction pitfalls made him an admirable chairman (1955–58) of the practice committee of the RIBA. He took a deep interest in the affairs of the NJCC of Architects, Quantity Surveyors and Builders. He was Master of the Art Workers Guild in 1956 and found time to act as a member of the school at Rome. He was elected ARA in 1955 and RA seven years later. He assessed the Golden-lane housing competition won by the then new firm of Chamberlin, Powell & Bon, which brought the first architectural 'new look' to the City of London.

He married in 1937 Margaret Cox and they have two sons and two daughters one of whom, Susan McMorran, is a valued contributor to 'The Builder.' To them we offer our deep sympathy.

IML [Ian Leslie, editor of the *Builder*] writes: By the death of Donald McMorran, the architectural profession loses more than it may as yet realise. A superb planner

Opposite: Window detail at Devon County Hall, Exeter, 1954–63

(he came from the Vincent Harris stable), McMorran suffered from being born into an architectural age which ran completely counter to his unshakeable belief that architecture derives from structure, and his consistent advocacy of this theme and his hard-hitting criticism of architectural education that, in his view, considered design as a thing apart from construction, could hardly be expected to make him a popular figure on a Board of Architectural Education which, as he saw it, indulged theory at the expense of practice. Resentments against the ideas expressed were responsible for the shelving of the report on education which, under his chairmanship, was produced in 1953 – a report which nevertheless paved the way for the Oxford Conference of architectural education, a conference which, notwithstanding, decided in favour of education centred on the universities and deliberately excluded the external student. Time will show which of the two arguments was right.

As a designer, McMorran was uneven. Even his most ardent supporters found it difficult to enthuse over some of his buildings, for example his façade to the building on the site of the Carlton Club in Pall Mall, or some of his collegiate work. But at their worst, his buildings have something of the grand manner, and at their best they have a quality of scale and proper use of traditional materials which will enable them to survive when some current flippant exercises in curtain walling come to be demolished. McMorran's exquisite police station in the Brook Green-road, Hammersmith, many feel to be the best building that never got a London Architecture medal – an award that came his way with two other buildings.

Busy in his practice, McMorran nevertheless found time to engage in battles either on behalf of architecture as an art or for any of his contemporaries whom he felt to be subjected to unfair pressures in the execution of their work. For some years he was a regular attender at RIBA annual general meetings where he drew attention to the then parlous state of Institute finances and urged retrenchment. The general run of Institute membership, eager for expansion at all costs, could not be expected to take kindly to a critic who quietly and remorselessly rubbed their nose in unpalatable financial fact, but McMorran was not a man who sought the plaudits of the crowd. Not surprisingly he enjoyed a number of deep personal friendships in which respect and affection found their part. It would have been a disappointment to him that he has not been spared to carry through, as Treasurer of the Royal Academy, the financial reforms needed by that ancient but somewhat creaking institution.

Builder, 13 August 1965

Obituary: George Whitby

Mr George Frederick Whitby, MBE, FRIBA, who was with his partner the late Donald H. McMorran, RA, architect for the 12 additional courts recently completed at the Old Bailey, died on February 22 at his Buckinghamshire home after a short illness. He was 56.

After leaving Ealing Grammar School, Whitby's studies at the Regent Street Polytechnic School of Architecture were interrupted by the war. He was in the Dunkirk evacuation, afterwards being commissioned in the Royal Engineers. He served in North Africa, and was wounded in the Desert. His work there on the assembly, under difficult conditions, of Bailey bridges brought him the MBE.

Demobilized at the end of the war as acting-Major, Whitby qualified as ARIBA and worked in the office of Welch, Cachemaille-Day and Lander before setting up in partnership with Walters and Kerr-Bate. In 1958 he joined Donald H. McMorran, sometime Treasurer of the Royal Academy, and assisted him in the important commissions which came to the firm – notably faculty buildings and halls of residence at Nottingham University; police headquarters at Wood Street, EC2, and Bury St Edmunds; county halls for Devon and Suffolk; and the offices on the site in Pall Mall of the old Carlton Club. Buildings on which Whitby was intimately concerned as architect were the Suffolk county hall, Bury St Edmunds; the Plashet county secondary school, West Ham; additions to Cranbrook School, Kent; and Queen Elizabeth School, Wakefield. He had been particularly concerned with the very large additions to the Central Criminal Court at the Old Bailey, completed only at the end of last year.

Whitby, an outgoing man who had served on RIBA committees and had helped in charitable work for his profession, married in 1946 Charmian Butler, and together they had four sons and two daughters.

The Times, 27 February 1973

Assistants at 14 North Audley Street

David Ancill
Ian Anderson
Mrs Maud Anstey
Raphäel Antille
Philip Beardsworth
Barry Boston
Frances Bourke
Steve Buscas
Miss Jane Campbell
(Farquharson &McMorran's secretary)
Roger Castle
Peter Church
John Collins
Hugh Connelly
David Crease
Ian Cruickshank
Tibor Cselko
Michael di Marco
Sydney Evans
Godfrey Grima
Derek Helme
Len Hobart
Roger Holden
Claude Ithier
Michael Katz
Ian Lennox
Jan Lubkowski
Robert McCleod
Alexander McMorran
Ruth Melamead
Ben Meredith

Alan Morgan
Alan Murnahan
Betty Murray
Jeanne Narborough
Danny Ng
David Nolan
Peter Nutall
Jim Peters
Lesley Porter
Ron Ringshall
Geoffrey Roberts
Yvonne Saville (Mrs Ward)
Duncan Sharpe
Peter Shew
Lawrence Slattery
Irene (Betty) Smallwood
Hilda Smith
Ray Smith
Christopher Southin
Peter Spurr
Elizabeth Stephenson
Ken Stott
Violet Telfer
Gordon Thompson
Norman Walker
Ian Waters
Alan Westbrook
Anita Wise
Ken Wrigglesworth
Robert Yap

McMorran & Whitby: Titles and positions held

Donald McMorran

ARIBA (1931)

FRIBA (1943)

FSA (1956)

Honorary Secretary of the Dorking and Leith Hill District Preservation Society

Joint Honorary Secretary of the RIBA Practice Committee (1947–52)

Honorary Secretary of the RIBA Competitions Committee (1947–51)

Member of the RIBA Visiting Board (1951–2)

Chairman of the RIBA Joint Committee on Architectural Education (1952–3)

Honorary Secretary of the RIBA Board of Architectural Education (1952–4)

ARA (1955)

Chairman of the RIBA Practice Committee (1955–8)

Master of the Art Workers Guild (1956)

Member of the Faculty of Architecture, British School at Rome

Member of the Joint Committee of London Architects and Builders

RA (1962)

Member of the Council of the Architects Benevolent Society

Member of the Artists' General Benevolent Institution

RIBA Representative on the National Joint Consultative Committee

Treasurer RA (1965)

RA Board of Architectural Education

Member of the Foreign Architectural Book Society

Member of the Athenaeum

Member of the Savile Club

George Whitby

MBE

ARIBA (1947)

FRIBA (1954)

RIBA Practice Committee (1947–56)

RIBA Official and Salaried Architects Committee (1949–60)

Member of the Reform Club

Member of National Joint Consultative Committee

'A Friendship'

The death of Whitby inspired a poem by his friend, poet Connie Bensley. Her poem, 'A Friendship', about George Whitby has received critical acclaim.

He made restless forays
into the edge of our marriage.
One Christmas Eve he came late,
his dark hair crackling with frost,
and ate his carnation buttonhole
to amuse the baby.
When I had a second child
he came to the foot of my bed at dusk
bringing pineapples and champagne,
whispering 'Are you awake?' –
singing a snatch of opera.
The nurse tapped him on the shoulder.
At the end, we took turns at his bedside.
I curled up in the chair; listened to each breath
postponing itself indefinitely.
He opened his eyes once and I leaned forward:
'Is there anything you want?'
'Now she asks,' he murmured.

Bibliography

Brian Appleyard, 'From God's house to Bauhaus and Back Again', *The Times*, 20–26 November 1982.

John Betjeman (Compiled & with an introduction by the Earl of Birkenhead), *John Betjeman's Collected Poems* (Enlarged Edition), John Murray (London, 1986).

H. A. N Brockman, 'Devon's New County Hall: An Essay in the Georgian', *Financial Times*, 14 July 1964, p10.

Nicholas Bullock, *Building the Post-War World: Modern Architecture and Reconstruction in Britain*, Routledge (London, 2002).

Mark Crinson & Jules Lubbock, *Architecture: Art or Profession? Three Hundred Years of Education in Britain*, Manchester University Press (1994).

A. Peter Fawcett & Neil Jackson, *Campus Critique: The Architecture of the University of Nottingham*, Sherwood Press (Nottingham, 1998).

Piero Gazzola, *Michele Sanmicheli: architetto veronese del Cinquecento*, Nero Pozzi Editore (Venice, 1960).

Mark Girouard, 'Creation or Pastiche? The Uses and Abuses of Classicism' (The Thomas Cubit Lecture), *Journal of the Royal Society of Arts*, January 1986, pp1-16.

Jeremy & Caroline Gould, 'Listed Building Management Guidelines for Devon County Hall', unpublished report, April 1999.

Brian Harvey, 'Early Industrial Architecture', *RIBA Journal*, July 1959, pp316–24.

Elain Harwood & Andrew Saint, *Exploring England's Heritage: London*, HMSO (Norwich, 1991).

Elain Harwood, *Something Worth Keeping? Post-War Architecture in England*, English Heritage (London, 1996).

Elain Harwood, *England: A Guide to Post-War Listed Buildings*, Second Edition, B. T. Batsford (London, 2003).

Paul Hindesmith, *A Composer's World: Horizons and Limitations* (Oxford, 1952).

Donald McMorran, Lecture notes, undated save where noted:
> 'Architecture in 1960', October 1960
> 'Everyday Things from the Architect's View Point'
> 'The Education of the Architect'
> 'The Value of Design in Rural Buildings'

Donald McMorran, Report on Pugin Tour, RIBA Drawings Collection at the V&A.

McMorran Report, *Architects' Journal*, 10 February 1955, p195.

Alan Powers, *Britain (Modern Architectures in History)*, Reaktion Books (London, 2007).

J. M. Richards, *The Functional Tradition in Early Industrial Buildings*, The Architectural Press (London, 1958)

A. E. Richardson, *Monumental Classic Architecture in Great Britain and Ireland during the Eighteenth and Nineteenth Centuries*, Batsford, (London, 1914)

Sparrow, W. Shaw, *The Modern Home; book of British domestic architecture for moderate incomes; a companion volume to "the British home of to-day"*, Hodder & Stoughton, (London, 1906), p159

Gavin Stamp, 'A Classicism beyond the "Battle of Styles"', *Independent*, 20 December 1989, p16.

Gavin Stamp, 'Classicism Without Columns', *The Persistence of the Classical*, Frank Salmon (ed.), Philip Wilson (London, 2008).

Gavin Stamp, 'McMorran and Whitby, A Progressive Classicism', *Modern Painters*, 4:4 (Winter 1991), pp56–60.

Rudolf Wittkower, *Architectural Principles in the Age of Humanism*, W. W. Norton & co. (London, 1952).

K. Wittmann & H. Gescheit, *Neuzeitlicher Verkehrsbau*, Muller & Kiepenheuer (Potsdam, 1931).

Letters by McMorran

'Deepdene Terrace Saved' [letter] *The Times*, 2 July, 1943, p4

'The A.S.B. and the "Tin Tacks" of Architectural Teaching', [letter], *RIBA Journal*, November 1948, pp37–8

'Buildings by St. Pauls' [letter], *The Times*, 4 June, 1953, p7

'Development Plan for Surrey' [letter], *The Times*, 11 May, 1954, p9

'Rebuilding the City' [letter] *The Times*, 27 January, 1954, p7

'Backward Readership', [letter], *RIBA Journal*, November, 1958, p28

'Architectural Taste' [letter], *The Times*, 20 November, 1959, p13

'History of the Immediate Future', [letter], *RIBA Journal*, July, 1961, p368

Index

Note: italic page numbers refer to illustrations

airports 16–19, 119–20
Amersham Free Church 95, *96*
Ancill, David 97
Art Workers Guild 99
Athenæum 99

Bailey, Arthur 14, 15–16, *15*
Battersea, Sir Walter St John's School 46–7
Bensley, Connie, poem 146
Bernard Sunley & Sons 50
Betjeman, John 3, 97–8, 110, 119
Board of Trade offices 13–14
Bow Road Open-Air School *43*, 44, 46
Bradford City municipal office buildings 15
Brandon-Jones, John 120
Braun, Hugh 6
Brian Colquhoun and Partners 119
Broadbent, E. R. 28
Brockman, H. A. N. 124
Brooke, Humphrey 99
Burnet, *Sir* John 24
Bury St Edmunds
    Library 89, *89*, 90, *91*
    police headquarters *88*, 89–90
    West Suffolk County Council offices 86–9,
        87, 90–2, *91*
Butler, Charmian 30

Camilla Lacy, private house *60*
Carlos Place 26
Carlton Club site 97–8, *98*
Central Criminal Court *94*, 95, 97, 114–19,
    115–16, *117–18*
Chamberlin, Powell & Bon 124
Chequer's Yard, Dorking 61, *61*
Chester, King's School *45*, 47
churches
    Amersham Free Church 95, *96*
    Coventry Cathedral *101–2*
    Northolt Grange 53
City of Bradford municipal office buildings 15

City Police Station 95, 97, 98, 102–9, *103–4*,
    105–6, *108*, 122, *144*
Clifton, Marshall 14, *15*
Cochrane, Raymond 30, 95
Conolly, Harold 47
Courtauld, Stephen 26
Coventry Cathedral 98, *101–2*
Cowell, Nigel 98
Cowles-Voysey, Charles 17
Cox, Margaret (wife of DM) 8, 16, 28
Cranbrook School 47
Creese, John 86
Cripps, Cyril and Humphrey 73–4, *74*
Cripps Hall, Nottingham University 72–80,
    74, *75–6*, *77–8*, *79*
Cselko, Tibor 92
Currie House, Poplar 36–40, *38*, *39*

Daily Mail Ideal Homes Competition *11*, 13
Denman, John 62
Devon County Hall 62–72, *63*, *64*, *65*, *67*, *70*
domestic works 11, *11*, *12*, 13, 129–31
    47 Grosvenor Square 26
    Fulmer, house 110
    Highworth, Wiltshire, manor 30
    Monks Risborough, Buckinghamshire *12*,
        13
    West Wycombe, estate cottages 99, *101*
    Westhumble, houses 60–1, *60*
Dorking, Chequer's Yard 61, *61*
Duke & Simpson 97
Dunkeld House, Poplar 36–40, *38*
Dyer, John 51

East Ham, Plashet County Secondary School
    for Girls 50–2, *51*
Ede, James Chuter 42
Ede House Police Section House, Hackney *32*,
    41, 42–4
Eden, William A. 124
Edgley, Ronald 110

Ellesmere Port and Whitby 15
Elliott, John Innes 42
Emerson, *Sir* William 13
Erith, Raymond 98, 120, 123
Evans, Sydney 98, *100*
Exeter, Devon County Hall 62–72, *63, 64, 65,*
    67, 70

Farquharson, David 111
Farquharson, Horace Cowley Nesham 1, 2, *2,*
    5, 30, 47, *119*
Farquharson, Noël *119*
Farquharson & McMorran 1, 3, 22–30, 33–45
Festival of Britain 14
Fitzroy Park 21
Folkstone Civic Centre 69, *71*
Foreign Architectural Book Society 99
Foster, Norman *4, 108*
Fulmer, house 110

Galbraith, R. F. 50
German design 19
Gibson & Russell 1
Godsall, H. G. 62
Golden Lane Estate 124
Goodhart-Rendel, H. S. 125
Greenwich Police Station and Section House
    10, 22, 26, *27–8*
Greyfriars Bridge, Hereford *96*
Grosvenor Square 26

Hackney, Ede House Police Section House 32,
    41, 42–4
Hall, Denis Clarke 53
Hammersmith College of Art 52
Hammersmith Police Station 23, 24–7, *25*
Hampstead
    Fellows Road 41
    Parkhill Housing Estate 33–5, *34, 35, 36*
Harlow, Purford Green County Infants and
    Junior Schools 44, 46
Harris, Alfred 51
Harris, Emanuel Vincent 2, 13, *14*, 17, 120
    house designed for 21, 22
Harvey, Brian 47, 105, 110
Harvey, James 13
Hereford, Greyfriars Bridge *96*

Highworth, Wiltshire, manor 30
Hodge, Frank 14, *15*
Holden, Charles 5, 54
Holford, *Sir* William 109
Holloway Road Housing Estate 111–13, *111–12*
Horder, Percy Morley 2, 13, 72
houses, private *see* domestic works
housing schemes 33–40
    Chequer's Yard, Dorking 61
    Currie House and Dunkeld House, Poplar
        36–40, *38, 39*
    Fellows Road, Hampstead 41
    Holloway Road Housing Estate 111–13,
        111–12
    Lammas Green Estate *48*, 57–60, *58–9*, 61
    Parkhill Housing Estate, Hampstead 33–5,
        34, 35, 37
    York Way Housing Estate, Islington 113, *113*
Hunstanton secondary school 53

Ideal Homes Competition *11*, 13
Indonesian Ambassador's Residence 53
Islington, York Way Housing Estate 113, *113*

Jellicoe, Geoffrey 73
John Player and Son, Nottingham 84–5, *85*

Kahn, Louis 114
King's School, Chester *45, 46*, 47

Lammas Green Estate *48*, 57–60, *58–9*, 61
Le Corbusier 17, 24, 77, 125
Leathart, Julian 62
Leicester, Wyggeston Grammar School 15,
    16
Lenton Hall, Nottingham University 83–4,
    83
Lewisham, Lammas Green Estate *48*, 57–60,
    58–9, 61
London County Council 13
'London's Future Airport' 16–19, *18*
Lutyens, *Sir* Edwin 1, 13, 17, 47, 76

Mallinson, Anne 116
Manchester Library and Town Hall extension
    15
Marylebone Police Station 23–4, *23*

McMorran, Alexander 84, 114, 120
McMorran, Donald 2, *15*, *16*, *29*
    architectural training 2, 6–8
    early career 2–3, 13, 15
    sketches *7–8*
    competition entries 11, *11*, 13, 15–20
    marriage and children 28–30, 49
    war years 30–1
    last years and death 110–11
    obituary 141–2
    portrait *110*
    titles and positions held 146
McMorran, Eleanor 29
McMorran, Margaret 28–9, *29*
McMorran, Peggy 16
McMorran, Susan 49
McMorran, William 84, 123
McMorran & Whitby
    assistants 85–6, 145
    legacy 123–6
    origin 1, 5, 49
    practice 54–5, 95, 111, 119, 120
McMorran and Bailey 15–16, *17*
McMorran House, Holloway 112, *112*
McMorran Report on education 54
Mendelsohn, Erich 19
Mid Glamorgan County Hall 13
Mies van der Rohe, Ludwig 19
Ministry of Defence 14
Mitchell, Tom 14, *15*
Modernism 19, 39, 57
Monks Risborough, Buckinghamshire, house
    12, 13
Moor Park, Hertfordshire 11
Mulberry Harbour 30
Murray, Betty *52*, 53, 95

Nairn, Ian 103–4
National Gallery extension 54, *55*
Neal, George 6
North Audley Street 1, 53, 95
Northolt Grange church 53
Nottingham, John Player and Son 84–5, *85*
Nottingham University
    Cripps Hall 72–80, *74*, *75–6*, *77–8*, *79*
    Lenton Hall 83–4, *83*
    Social Science Building 80–3, *81*, *82*

Pall Mall 97–8, *98*
Parkhill Housing Estate, Hampstead 33–5, *34*,
    35, *37*
Perth, University of Western Australia 15
Peters, Jim 111, 113
Phoenix School *43*, 44, 46
Pierce, Stephen Rowland 62
Plashet County Secondary School for Girls
    50–2, *51*
police stations 22–7
    Bury St Edmunds *88*, 89–90
    Ede House Police Section House, Hackney
        32, 42–4
    Greenwich Police Station and Section
        House *10*, 22, 26, 27–8
    Marylebone Police Station 23–4, *23*
    Wood Street Police Station 98, *100*, 102–9,
        103–4, *105–6*, *108*, 122, *144*
Poplar
    Currie House 36–40, *38*, *39*
    Dunkeld House 36–40, *38*
Powell, Geoffry 124
private houses *see* domestic works
public buildings 132–7 (*see also* housing
    schemes; police stations; school buildings)
    100 Pall Mall 97–8, *98*
    Devon County Hall 23, 57, 62–72, *63*, *64*,
        65, *67*, *70*
    Folkstone Civic Centre 69, *71*
    Indonesian Ambassador's Residence 53
    Swiss Embassy 53
    West Suffolk County Council offices 86–9,
        87, *88*, 90–2, *91*
    York, Municipal Offices 19–21, *20*, *21*
Purchase, Edward Keynes 13
Purford Green County Infants and Junior
    Schools 44, 46

Queen Elizabeth's School, Wakefield 47

Ramboll Whitbybird 52
Regent Street Polytechnic 6, 11
residences *see* domestic works
RIBA
    DM's professional involvement 99, 141
    Joint Committee on Architectural
        Education 54

London Architecture Bronze Medal 27, 46
Pugin Travelling Studentship 8
Royal Gold Medal 14
Ringshall, Ron 108
Rogers, Richard *4*, *108*
Royal Academy 98, 99, 100

Sanmicheli, Michele 107, 125
Scandinavian design 125
school buildings
    Bow Road Open-Air School *43*, 44, 46
    Cranbrook School 47
    Hunstanton secondary school 53
    King's School, Chester *45*, *46*, 47
    Plashet County Secondary School for Girls, East Ham 50–2, *51*
    Purford Green County Infants and Junior Schools, Harlow 44, 46
    Queen Elizabeth's School, Wakefield 47
    Sir Walter St John's School, Battersea 46–7
    St Paul's Choir School 54–7, *56*
    Wyggeston Grammar School, Leicester 15, 16
Seely, John 55
Shearing, Arthur 97
Simmonds, Posy 107
Sir Walter St John's School 46–7
Smithson, Alison and Peter 53
Southern Wood, Westhumble *60*
Spence, *Sir* Basil 84, 98–9
Spragg, C. D. 62
St Paul's Choir School 54–7, *56*
St Paul's Watch 30
Stamp, Gavin 102
Stokes, Leonard 13
Swansea Civic Buildings 15, 16
Swiss Embassy 53
Sydenham Hill, Lammas Green Estate *48*, 57–60, *58–9*, 61

Tait & Lorne 24
Tempest, Stanley 8
Thomas, *Sir* Percy 73
Tonbridge Civic Centre 92
Toy, Sydney 95
Trench, George Mackenzie 23

unbuilt projects 137–9
University of Western Australia 15
Uren, Reginald 92

Vine & Vine 24
Voysey, Charles 13

W. V. Zinn & Associates 66
Wakefield, Queen Elizabeth's School 47
Walker, Norman *52*, 111
Walters, Whitby & Kerr Bate 49
Walters & Kerr Bate 3, 49
Watson, John 14, *15*
Welch, Cachemaille-Day & Lander 3
West Suffolk County Council offices 86–9, *87*, *88*, 90–2, *91*
West Wycombe, estate cottages 99, *101*
Westhumble, Surrey, private houses 60–1, *60*
Wheeler, *Sir* Charles 99, 100
Whitby, Charmian (*née* Butler) 30, 52
Whitby, George 2, 3, *52*, 120
    architectural training 3
    war years 30
    early career 49–53
    marriage and children 52
    death 119, 146
    titles and positions held 146
    obituary 143
Whitby, Mark 52, 118
Whitby, Richard 118
Whitby & Bird 52
Whitby Court 113
Wimbledon Municipal Offices and Assembly Hall 15
Wolverhampton Assembly Halls 15, *17*
Wood Street Police Station 98, *100*, 102–9, *103–4*, *105–6*, *108*, 122, *144*
Worthington, *Sir* Hubert 62
Wyggeston Grammar School, Leicester 15, 16

Yap, Robert 120
York, Municipal Offices 19–21, *20*, *21*
York Way Housing Estate, Islington 113, *113*

Zinn (W. V.) & Associates 66

Picture Credits

The author and publisher have made every effort to contact copyright holders and will be happy to correct, in subsequent editions, any errors or omissions that are brought to their attention.

© The Art Workers Guild p110

Betty Murray p52 (bottom)

Charmian Smith p112

David Farquharson p2 (top left and top right), p119

© Edward Denison Frontispiece, ppx, xiii, xiv, 4, 10, 22, 23 (bottom), 26 (both), 32, 37 (both), 38 (both), 39, 40, 41, 49, 51, 58 (both), 61, 64, 65 (both), 68 (both), 70 (top left, bottom left, bottom right), 75, 76, 77, 78, 81, 82 (top) , 85, 88 (bottom), 91 (both), 94, 96 (top left), 98, 104 (all), 108, 112 (top), 113, 115 (top), 117 (all), 122, 128, 133, 135, 136, 140, 144

Eric de Maré pp43, 67

G.L.Ward p96 (bottom)

John A. Rose cover photo, p103

John Gay pp111, 116

John Laing & Son Ltd back cover photo, p79

© Kings School pp45, 46

Mark Whitby p2 (bottom right)

From the McMorran family archive pp2 (bottom left), 7, 8 (both), 12 (both), 14, 15, 16, 17, 18 (both), 20 (both), 21, 23 (top), 25 (both), 29, 35, 55, 56 (both), 59 (both), 60, 63 (both), 70 (top left), 71 (both), 79, 88 (top), 101 (bottom), 105 (top), 106, 112 (bottom), 130

McMorran & Whitby office p115 sketch by Arthur Shearing

Reproduced by permission of English Heritage.NMR pp83, 89

© RIBA Library Drawings Collection pp8 (both), 11, 34, 45, 82 (bottom), 96 (top right), 100, 102, 105 (bottom)

© Royal Academy of Arts, London p101 (top)

© Suffolk County Council p87 (both)

© The Nottingham Evening Post p74